Presented To:

_____

From:

_____

Date:

_____

HEAVEN IS
BEYOND
YOUR
WILDEST
EXPECTATIONS

DESTINY IMAGE BOOKS BY SID ROTH

Stories of Supernatural Healing (with Linda Josef Ph.D.)

Supernatural Experiences

Supernatural Healing (with Linda Josef Ph.D.)

The Incomplete Church

There Must Be Something More!

They Thought for Themselves

Truth Seekers (with Mike Shreve)

HEAVEN IS BEYOND *YOUR* WILDEST *EXPECTATIONS*

Ten True Stories of Experiencing Heaven

SID ROTH
& LONNIE LANE

DESTINY IMAGE® PUBLISHERS, INC.
P.O. Box 310, Shippensburg, PA 17257-0310
"Promoting Inspired Lives"

This book and all other Destiny Image, Revival Press, Mercy-Place, Fresh Bread, Destiny Image Fiction, and Treasure House books are available at Christian bookstores and distributors worldwide.

For a U.S. bookstore nearest you, call 1-800-722-6774.
For more information on foreign distributors, call 717-532-3040.
Reach us on the Internet: www.destinyimage.com.

ISBN 13 TP: 978-0-7684-0286-5
ISBN 13 Ebook: 978-0-7684-8803-6

For Worldwide Distribution, Printed in the U.S.A.
1 2 3 4 5 6 7 / 15 14 13 12

DEDICATION

To all who hope for Heaven, may you find the assurance you seek in these pages.

ACKNOWLEDGMENT

My thanks to Sid Roth for the opportunities he has provided for me, for his partnership in this book, and for being a man who is committed to always doing God's will. –Lonnie Lane

*The heavens will praise Your wonders,
O Lord; Your faithfulness also in the
assembly of the holy ones.*

—Psalm 89:5.

CONTENTS

FOREWORD

As a young Jewish boy, I remember being home in bed late at night alone. A strange question continually crossed my mind, *What will happen to me when I die?* We Jews most definitely believe in life after death, but my parents had never discussed this with me.

My logical sequence of thoughts went like this, *If I die, I will cease to exist.* Then I tried to imagine what it would be like if I ceased to exist. The more I exercised my vivid imagination, the more objectionable my thoughts became. Whatever was "me" I didn't want "me" to be snuffed out. So I did the only sensible thing I could do. I stopped thinking about it and blocked it from my mind till many years later.

At age twenty-nine I had an early mid-life crisis and death looked better to me than my life did. At a moment of great crisis, I did the only thing left to do, I cried out to God for help. And suddenly He was there! I knew instantly He was real and that the Bible account about Heaven and hell was true.

Up to this point, I have never visited Heaven. However, I have interviewed many who have had Heaven and hell visitations. Frankly, for me, it is not necessary; but I still wish I could visit Heaven and see it before I die. Those whom God has selected to be living witnesses on earth of the glory of Heaven provoke me to jealousy.

I remember in the early '70s interviewing Dr. Richard Eby. He was a medical doctor who died and went to Heaven, then lived to tell about it. Because of his amazing memory, he made me feel I was experiencing Heaven also. Then, over the years I have interviewed many more people who had heavenly visitations. Their stories all had many similar ingredients and none of them wanted to return to earth. They all longed to stay in Heaven.

In recent years, the number of visitations has increased dramatically. Why? The Messiah is getting ready to come to earth. I believe when you read this book it will make you more heavenly minded than earthbound. It will give you a glimpse of the love God has for you beyond anything you have imagined until now, and it will give you a wonderful picture of your glorious and eternal future. It will bring you such a supernatural peace that it will grow daily; and this peace will overpower the cares of this life.

You were created to taste the rarified air of Heaven, even while still here on earth. Enjoy!

Shalom and love,
SID ROTH

INTRODUCTION

Welcome to our world, where the natural is naturally supernatural! Sid Roth and I share the longing for every person, Jew or Gentile, to know the wonders of life with Messiah Jesus (in Hebrew, Yeshua), not only in this life but forever! Do you have an assurance of your eternal destiny? Read these stories and have your ideas of Heaven explode into fireworks of brilliance and glory in the truth presented in them. I guarantee that you will never see life, especially your eternal life, the same way ever again.

These stories give you an opportunity to see into the heavenly realm perhaps even beyond what His disciples understood about Heaven at that time and even about Jesus as the Lord of all that exists, for we know so much more of the universe today than they did. Perhaps we are being given the greatest privilege of any generation to know what awaits us in eternity. Why is that?

On Sid's television show, *It's Supernatural!,* Sid has interviewed a number of people who have been to Heaven and to hell and returned to tell about it. One man, Bruce Allen, told of meeting his aunt in Heaven who had died seven years earlier. She told him that Heaven is abuzz and excited because the culmination of all things is coming and many individuals are visiting Heaven now and being sent back to tell the people on the earth of the validity of Heaven, and the message that the Lord is coming back very soon. How soon is very soon? Only God knows, but we are exhorted to make ourselves ready to meet Him whenever He comes. God has also made us aware that hell is as real as Heaven but that it is not His will that any should go there. The choice is ours as you will see in some of the stories you are about to read.

It is our hope that as a result of reading this book you will see the challenges that life offers us here on the earth as momentary light afflictions compared to the glory that awaits us in Heaven, *"for momentary, light affliction is producing for us an eternal weight of glory far beyond all comparison"* (2 Cor. 4:17). When we know that splendor and glory is our eternal destiny, we can endure whatever we must while patiently waiting for the day when we too enter Heaven and our eternal joy in the presence of the Lord.

As you read the stories of what these people experienced, keep an open ear for what God might want to tell you about Himself or what He might want to say to you. You might even want to keep a notebook near you to jot down things you feel God might be saying to you or thoughts you may want to remember. Use this book not just as something to read, but as your own opportunity to experience a taste of Heaven from here on earth.

Blessings upon you!
LONNIE LANE

CHAPTER 1

EXPERIENCING THE THRONE OF GOD

by Dean Braxton

Dean died in the hospital. Three times he came before Jesus but each time Jesus sent him back saying, "It is not your time." This time he hoped to stay.

It was wonderful to be going to where Jesus is. I was not looking for anyone else but Jesus. I knew where I was going. I was moving super fast. As the Bible says, I was absent from my body and heading for the presence of the Lord. I was moving faster than it takes you to read the next sentence. I was immediately in the presence of my Lord.

From the first moment I was in Heaven there was the continual sound of praise and worship. The atmosphere seemed to be filled with a continuous musical sound. It was constant and like no other sound I know. I was more than just hearing it. I was experiencing it. The closest I can come to describing it is like when you can feel drum beat vibrations. Praise was always there in the atmosphere.

When I first arrived in Heaven and knelt before Jesus, all I could do was say, "You did this for me? Thank You, thank You, thank You!" Everything in me cried out in praise to Jesus. It was pure joy. Jesus is pure light! His brightness was before me, around me, part of me, and in me. He is brighter than the noonday sun, but we can still look at Him in Heaven. It seemed to me that if someone was not right with Him, that person would be burned up by this brightness. But those who were right with Him could look at Him and have perfect joy. If you were not right with Him, then terror would be what you would experience. You have to look at Him with a pure heart.

His Body of Love

Jesus is more beautiful, wonderful, and glorious than I can explain. I stopped looking at Him with my eyes and saw Him as He is—from my heart. I was on my hands and knees as I looked into His face. How do I tell you what His face looks like? His face was as if it were liquid crystal glass made up of pure love, light, and life. From His face came the colors of the rainbow and colors

I cannot describe inside His being. All these colors were part of Jesus and they were coming out from His being as the waves of the ocean come to the seashore. He is not a color as we know colors. I was seeing the colors, and I was part of the colors. I was in the colors, and the colors were coming out of me. I was seeing Jesus, and I was part of Jesus. I was in Jesus, and Jesus was shining out of me. I would see the brightness. The brightness was around me. I was part of the brightness, and brightness was shining out of me. All of it was life. I just wanted to praise Him forever.

I was seeing Jesus, and I was part of Jesus.

If you know Jesus as your Lord and Savior, you will outlive every problem you will ever face on this earth. That is Good News! Everything about Jesus is love. His love for you is so personal it seems as if it is only for you. You come to realize that He has cared for you forever and will continue to care for you forever. His love is alive. It is more than just a sense. You are becoming His love. You are His love. Jesus loves us completely.

I saw various parts of His body, and each part seemed to love me. I saw His feet. He still has the wounds where the nails pierced His feet. But what really overwhelmed me was the love His feet showed me. He loved me so much that I did not have to look at His face to experience the love He has for me. Even His feet expressed His love for me. It was not only that He loved me, but it was like I was the only one He loved in all of His creation. I knew He loved others, but it seemed as if I was the only one. His feet loved me!

When I looked at His hands, I experienced the same love. I could see the nail piercings, but it was the love that was coming out of them *to* me that expressed His love *for* me. As I looked at other parts of His body, I experienced over and over again, the love of Jesus just for me. I came to understand that He advocates for us with His whole being. I saw what His body went through just for me. I saw what it cost Him for me to be there and to have a relationship with God Almighty. I did not know before this happened how much it cost in pain to His physical body for us to have a relationship with God. He still bears the scars of what He suffered for us.

On His head was a crown that looked like the sun in all its glory with rays going up and out in the atmosphere of Heaven. I could not see any end to the rays. I knew the rays had something to do with healing. The rays intertwined with His hair. His head and hair were white like wool, as white as snow. As I looked at His hair and crown, I again experienced His love for me.

Heaven is huge and expanding. Our universe is like a fragment compared to Heaven. I came to understand that Heaven is expanding, becoming larger. There is no distance, as we know it here on earth. I seemed to be far from things and yet near. If I wanted to be somewhere else in Heaven I just had to think it, and I was there.

The most gorgeous sky ever seen here on earth cannot even come close to the atmosphere in Heaven. It is bright because of the glory of our God. Jesus and the Father light up everything. There is no darkness in Heaven. Their glory, or light, shines out of everything. The atmosphere is something you experience, not just see. It is golden, yellow, white, and had more colors moving throughout it. The atmosphere looked like curtains moving on a breezy day. It also looked like a waterfall in reverse. It was as if I was looking at one of the great waterfalls on this earth and seeing the water going up the fall, not down. I first came to really see how alive the atmosphere was when it bowed when Jesus spoke to me. It just folded over and bowed.

Jesus' words are alive! Jesus spoke to me with His voice. His voice is love. His voice is mighty. His voice left Him with power and authority, but when it got to me, it was life and comfort—especially for me! It was alive when it entered into me. The words He spoke to me were from His heart, just like everything else there. When Jesus and the Father, or other beings wanted to communicate, generally they did so through thought only. Because everything is alive, everything can communicate so that you "experience" the communication—you don't just hear it. There was no miscommunication, no mis-understandings. There was nothing you would hide from one another. We were all pure, so every thought was pure. There was a rule that you did not go into any other's thoughts without them giving you permission to do so. The last being that did that was Lucifer and he is no longer there in Heaven.

Everyone and everything praised the Lord; but the only time I saw beings open their mouths, was when they were singing praises to the Father at the throne. Every living being and creature praises the Father and Jesus. Every part of God's creation praises God all the time. No one else receives praise, only God. Worship is like breathing air here on earth. I seemed to live off the praise. I lived because of God Himself and nothing else. I did not need any food. Praising Him seems to be all that is needed. To hear the flowers praise the Lord is won-derful. The birds sing praise to the Lord. Water praised the Lord. Mountains praised the Lord. Praise came from the atmosphere and praise was in the atmosphere. Praise was the atmosphere! We all praised Him repeatedly, over and over again. We never ran out of things for which to praise Him.

When I looked into Jesus' eyes, His eyes were like flames of fire with changing colors of red, orange, blue, green, yellow, and many other colors. John said in

Revelation 1:14 that, *"His eyes were like a flame of fire."* I experienced in His eyes that they are deep and full of life. I could get lost in His eyes and never want to come out. In His eyes I saw the love for every human and creation of God. At first it seemed as if His eyes had love only for me. But when I thought about someone else, I saw His love for that person. It was like He loved only that person. So I thought about someone else, and the same thing happened. I saw His love for that other person. I did this with a number of heavenly beings and a few people here on earth. I saw in His eyes that He wanted everyone who is still alive on this earth to be in Heaven in due time. He did not want to lose one person or have them go to hell. Jesus wants all people saved.

When I looked in His eyes and saw this love, I knew I became that love also. If we have Jesus, we have His love in us and should be becoming His love for others. He loves us no matter what! Now, during that time of looking into His eyes, we communicated through our thoughts—no words were spoken. I said to Him, "Even child molesters?" I had worked with children and teenagers over the past 33 years. During that time, the one issue that came up a lot with the children I had worked with was sexual abuse by adults. This one issue, to me, seems to do more damage than all the other issues I faced as a counselor. I have seen many people who had recovered from many types of abuse, but every time I had to deal with someone who had been sexually abused, the damage seemed to be the most harmful out of all the other abuses. I would always get upset inside myself.

So as we communicated, Jesus said to me, "When you place a person in jail, they get out. They either get out when their time is up, or they get out when they die, but they get out. But when we put a person in hell, they are there for eternity." Then His eyes looked at me with a fiery red flame that said, "WHO ARE YOU TO NULIFY WHAT I HAD DONE!" This came across to me as very stern. I saw Him stretch out His arms like He was on the cross where He paid the price for everyone who has or ever will sin, implying that we do not have a right to condemn anyone since He does not. He truly wants all people there with Him. *All* people! But it is for each person to accept His atoning death for his or her sins in order to enter the newness of life He offers to us.

One of the most fascinating things I experienced was being connected to everything there at the same moment. It is like the electricity that connects power to run anything that needs electric energy here. It is like our computer systems that are connected to the Internet, which connects us to every computer in the world. God connects every one of His creations together. Because of this, I came to understanding life in Heaven quickly. There is no substance on earth that can come close to what substance God used to create everything in Heaven. There is no sin to corrupt what God has made.

His creations there are in their purest form. There is no sin to destroy what God has made.

THE ARMY OF GOD

I came to understand there are two units in the army of God. There is a heavenly unit and earthly unit, but they are the same army of God. The heavenly unit is made up of the angels of God. The heavenly unit understands for whose Kingdom they work. When Jesus would communicate to them, they showed great awe and respect. That moment for me, I have not forgotten. I wanted to be with His creation that honored Him for who He is, the King of kings and the Lord of lords. I saw how those heavenly creatures bowed before they left Him, and backed out as they left. They would not turn their backs to Him. They left immediately on their assignment. They were sent to fight in the heavenly realms. They were fighting evil spirits that belong to Satan's army. I knew that prayer is what moved them.

Then, there is the earthly unit, the one I was sent back to join. I left as a soldier going to war. I knew that it would be for a short time and my life on this earth would be short-lived. If I stay here on earth another 50 to 100 years, it is short compared to eternity. I want to be part of this unit here on earth as long as I can. I know what the heart of God is. It is to get people saved. It is to get people to live with Him forever.

A River of Prayers

If I were to die right now, I would be in Heaven in a twinkling of an eye. Yet the prayers of people who were praying for me and other prayers were moving faster than I was when I was on my way to Heaven. They were like shooting stars passing me. All I saw as they went by me were balls that looked like fire and a tail of light that looked like fire. I saw prayers as I was going to Heaven and prayers as I was coming back to my body in the hospital on earth. I was moving in a river of prayers going to Heaven. The prayers close to me were for me; the farther away the prayers were from me, they were for other people.

Just think, if you were praying at the time I left my body to go to Heaven, I saw your prayer pass me by. It passed me as if I was standing still. I knew there were two types of prayers passing me. One type was prayers from people who had prayed a prayer and understood the authority they had when they prayed the prayer. They were praying in faith from their hearts. They were praying according to a verse in the Bible that they had understanding of. They were praying the will of God over me and others. So when they prayed it, they knew in their heart what it was supposed to do. And they knew that God would answer the prayer with His power.

When I arrived in Heaven, I went to the feet of Jesus and stopped there. The prayers went straight to the throne and the Father. Not only did they go to Father God, they went inside Him. To try to understand this, you will have to realize that the throne of God is not a seat. It is a place. Well, more than that. He *is* the Throne! There were millions upon millions of prayers entering the Father. Our prayers became Him, and He became our prayers. I saw these lights of prayers like shooting stars entering the Father. I came to understand that He answers our prayers with Himself.

I came to understand that He answers our prayers with Himself.

Jesus downloaded information into me about prayers. I understood that our prayers must come from our hearts. Our God is a heart God, and He is looking for us to talk to Him from our hearts. I do not have the word to describe this, but our prayers become substances. They only become substances if we are praying to God from our hearts. He hears us if we are praying from our hearts. He hears your heart. He understands your heart. He only hears prayers from the heart.

I saw Jesus strategizing; He knelt down to the ground and put His hand out pointing at the ground and the ground rose up and became a city. What city I could not tell you. I just knew it was an earthly city. He pointed at areas in the city and looked up at an angel. He bowed and backed out quickly. I knew the angel had been given instruction on what to do. I knew that Jesus had received information about a situation on earth that the Father had gotten from someone praying here on earth and gave that information to Jesus—at the same moment He had received the information. Then Jesus saw what the Father wanted and gave that information to the angels that went to earth to carry out the orders that were given to them by Jesus.

GOD THE FATHER

I want to attempt to describe Father God as I saw Him there in Heaven. God the Father is as the Bible says, a Spirit. He is pure Spirit. He is pure Love and He is pure Life and He is pure Light! That is who He is. I connect everything that God does back to who He is—Love, Life, and Light. He cannot come at us any other way than what He is. All that He does comes out of who He is. He is very vast, as in never-ending. The word "big" does not come close to describing what I saw or experienced. The angels that fly around Him saying, "Holy, holy, holy" are very small compared to God. He has the form of a human. Or better yet, we have the form of God. We look like Him. We were made after His likeness.

I really cannot wrap my thinking around Him. He is large, huge, vast, infinite, enormous, immeasurable, unrestricted, unrestrained, never-ending, endless, without end, free and at liberty to be God. I really have not found words in English to describe God. I have no thought to even grasp what I saw. All I can say is there is no end to God the Father. He is bright like Jesus with many colors coming off of Him. Jesus and the Father God light up everything. They do not let any darkness in Heaven. None at all! Every being there has God the Father and Jesus inside of them. They live outside of every being and inside every being. Every being shines because of the Father and Jesus. They are the light within every living being and creature. Darkness has nowhere to hide.

When I saw Father God sitting on the Throne, another of my ideas of God was blown up. He was sitting on the throne yet He *is* the Throne, as I said earlier. God is vast and the throne was God, and God was the throne. He had colors coming from Him, more colors than I can tell you. The colors were alive just as everything that comes from God the Father is alive. Before the Throne there was an immeasurable number of heavenly creatures giving God praise. He was in the midst of the Throne and connected to the Throne. Where He was, the Throne was there. I had always believed God was sitting on a chair, but that was not so. The Throne was bright and looked like a cloud. What I experienced about the Throne was that God the Father was and has never been separated from the Throne. It was hard for me to take in all that I experienced before the Throne of God. God says in Isaiah that, *"Heaven is My throne and the earth is My footstool"* (Isa. 66:1). This Throne was God Himself. Who could make a Throne for God, but God?

As I looked at the Throne, I saw how much the Father loves us. I knew Jesus loved us very much, but to see the Father's love for us—*wow!* I looked into His eyes. When I did, all I could think was, *I don't know how many universes you can place in His eyes.* But out of all that I saw, what really stood out to me was the love that He has for each and every one of us on earth.

I came to understand that every time we take a breath of air, the Father God is saying, "I love you." The only reason air is here, is for you. There is no other reason that the air is here. How many times in a day do you take a breath of air? Whatever the number is how many times God is telling you that He loves you. Hear Him as you breathe say, "I love you."

I understood that there is no number two in God's eyes. Everyone is number one. There is no one taking the place of number two, three, four, five, six, seven, eight, nine, or the tenth person. There is only number one, everyone is number one to Him. Everyone is first in line with Him. There is no difference even here on earth. If you know Jesus as Lord and Savior, you are number one to Him. As the Bible says, we are the apple of His eye.

I was on my hands and knees when I saw the Throne. I was far and yet I was near the Throne of God. The innumerable beings that surrounded the Throne were giving Him praise. Some had been human beings from earth and others were heavenly beings. Between them and the Throne was something like water. It looked like a crystal sea, but it was not. It was something like water, but not really. Now after this crystal-like sea, there was another liquid under the Throne of God. The Throne hovers over this liquid, which was also alive. It had a different density to it compared to the crystal-like sea. These two liquids flowed through each other, but did not overlap or blend or bleed into each other. They stayed very much separate. I have not found the words to really describe the beauty of these water-like liquids. All I can say is that they were alive and had a personality to them. Throughout Heaven there are more water-like liquids that are alive and have delightful personalities.

Worship

As I saw and listened to worship before my Father's Throne, I heard a sound so beautiful that it has changed my worship of God forever. This part that I am about to tell you changed my life the most here on earth. I experienced something about God the Father that changed the way I look at life altogether. When you, as a pure spirit being, get to look at the Father, you see Him completely different from how you have previously perceived Him to be. Let me attempt to tell you what I am talking about. I pray that the heart of your understanding is open to receive what I have come to know about our Father God.

Before the Throne, after I saw all that I just told you, I heard another sound that I had a hard time accepting when I got back to earth. It was a sound that I knew brought me life, and life more abundantly. This sound was God the Father singing back to each and every being giving Him praise before the Throne. He was singing an individual love song to each of His creations. The song was alive and seemed to go inside of the beings it was meant for. What I saw was just like in the Song of Songs in the Bible. There is an exchange of love words between God and each person expressing his or her love for one another. That is what was going on in Heaven. Father God was expressing His love for each being and they were expressing their love for Him.

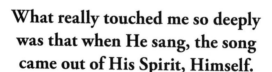

**What really touched me so deeply
was that when He sang, the song
came out of His Spirit, Himself.**

I now believe that happens to us here on earth when we express our love to God. I have not tried to copy His song. What really touched me so deeply was that when He sang, the song came out of His Spirit, Himself.

The song was not touched by any other creation of His. Nothing in Heaven stopped it or would think to stop His song from reaching the targeted being. With the songs from the beings to the Father who sits on the Throne, the crystal-like sea had its part and the colors had their part. But when it came to God's song, no one had a part but Him and the being it was meant for. This song was pure love. I understood by seeing this love song come from the Father, in the power of His love.

I knew that not only was the Father sending a love song to each and every creation of His in Heaven, but also on earth. He is sending love to all people on the planet. All the time love from God is being sent out to each and every person, and nothing can stop this love from reaching us. We can deny His love, reject His love, or act like His love is not there, but He keeps sending it to us. Every time we take a breath of air, He is saying, "I love you." When you now take a breath of air, listen to the Father telling you that He loves you. *"For God so loved the world"* (John 3:16) became more alive to me in seeing and hearing this love song from the Father to each being there.

Jesus wanted me to make sure when I tell my story that everyone I talk to knows that this is not our home; we who know Jesus as Lord and Savior are just passing through. It seemed to me that this earth was just a small part of a very big picture, a really small part. This earth is deteriorating. We are in a countdown to the end of the age. But we seem to think and act as if this is our home forever. Yet Jesus told us that He goes to prepare a place for us (see John 14:2). He was not talking about a house or a mansion as we say many times, but a much greater place in Heaven just for us. When I was there, I knew that I was in my place and no one else could take it. It was prepared for me. I also knew that I was not taking anyone else's place. When I talk about the music there, I understood that each being's song had its own place. I knew I was in my place and no one could take it away. Jesus has a place in Heaven just for you, where you will know Him completely as Lord and Savior. It was made just for you—no one else.

Commentary

The most life-changing aspect of Dean's visit to Heaven is the depth of God's love that Dean experienced over and over again. It wasn't just God's love as a fact, it was God's love *for him*—as if Dean was the only object of God's love, yet knowing God loves everyone in His creation the same way. When Dean was in the presence of the Lord Jesus, Dean felt His love coming from every part of Jesus' anatomy. The Lord not only loves, He *is* love. It's not just His heart or mind that loves us, it's every part of Him. You can see how His love for us has nothing to do with what we do or refrain from doing. Once we receive His unconditional love, it dispels any kind of rule keeping, works, or behaviors to try to gain or keep God's favor. When we know we have His love like this, sin loses any appeal it might have had. Who can be anything but entirely secure knowing God's love like this? Further, it also washes away any fear of rejection by God we might have once we know there is nothing in Him that cannot or will not love us.

Once we know we are altogether, entirely loved, and fully accepted by Him, we lose all interest in the things of this world that might have drawn us away from Him or His holiness. We love Him because He first loves us. The response to His love, His greatness, and His glory evokes a spontaneous, continual loving worship of Him from every created being in Heaven. Even the flowers in Heaven worship God, and the very atmosphere bows in worship before Him. But even more wonderful is that as each worships God in song, He responds to each person's worship and sings a personal love song back to each person—there is an exchange of love between the Father and each of His beloved. We might know what it is to be deeply in love with someone who loves us in return, but God has given that to us as but a mere shadow of the reality of His love.

What we often have difficulty saying, we can easily sing. God has created us, even our brains, to function this way. Sing your prayers to God and then be aware as you are singing to Him of what He is singing back to you. Allow God to wrap you in His love for you. It is a life changer!

For as high as the heavens are above the earth, So great is His lovingkindness toward those who fear [revere] *Him* (Psalm 103:11).

About Dean Braxton

Dean and his wife, Marilyn, are licensed ministers and travel the United States sharing the Good News of Jesus the Messiah. They have also been invited to speak about Dean's heavenly experience, supported with Scripture, on numerous television shows. Marilyn talks about her experience through the prayer that brought Dean back to life. Their mission is to share how much God loves us and to give hope in a unique and transparent way. Dean is the author of *In Heaven: Experiencing the Throne of God.*

CHAPTER 2

JOURNEY OF GLORY

by Rhoda "Jubilee" Mitchell

Things were not going well for twenty-year-old Jubilee. She was overwhelmed with defeat. She cried out to God in her despair and suddenly Jesus, who is a very present help in trouble, came to her and lifted her not just from depression but out of her body to reveal to her that what she was feeling isn't all there is; there is so much more! That day, the spirit realm became very real to her.

The last thing I remember was lying face down on my bed. I was repeating to God over and over "I can't take it any more, I just can't take it any more." I knew the Bible says, "Whoever will call upon the name of the Lord will be saved." So I cried out to God and something amazing happened! Jesus immediately appeared next to me. He came to rescue me.

Suddenly I could see myself lying face down on the bed. My spirit had been separated from my body. Then all at once Jesus and I flew up into the sky. He flew me up through the roof of my home. When we got about twelve feet above the roof, I looked down toward my bedroom. I saw the tiles on the top of the roof, but the roof was transparent. I could see clear through it. My eyesight had been changed. It was heightened along with all of the rest of my senses.

Immediately after Jesus took me out of my body, my consciousness was acutely aware of my surroundings. It was as if I had been awakened from a deep sleep. I was totally renewed. My mind was refreshed and alert. I felt more alive than I had ever felt before. I became keenly aware that my normal limitations were being removed. My body was no longer hindered by solid material. I could see through walls as well as sail through them. People go through a change that happens after death; it is as if we become completely new creatures.

As Jesus and I ascended into the night sky, the heavens became dark and filled with stars. The celestial vista was breathtaking. As we continued flying through the night sky, I distinctly remember that the moon was arcing to the north and left as we sailed upward to the right. I was awestricken. The feeling of peace in Jesus' arms was amazing!

I became aware of God and Jesus communicating with each other. They were "thinking" to each other, but in my mind it was a distinct dialogue. They could hear each other's thoughts, and I could sense how much they love one another. As I listened to God and Jesus talking to each other, many things flooded through my mind. I was able to witness the Godhead working together in complete harmony. I was beholding the "ultimate love relationship." It was incredible!

God's Universe

Here I was, experiencing firsthand the wonders of God's universe. The sheer expanse of the heavens unfolded in a beautiful array of glistening stars and shining planets and the love of God shone brightly through every sparkle of each twinkling light. God's love was a tangible presence. The scientist inside of me died, and the lover emerged. God's love began shooting through me like arrows aimed directly at my heart. His love surrounded me. His affection encircled me. It flowed over me like the waves of a great ocean.

I was experiencing firsthand the wonders of God's universe.

When Jesus separated my spirit from my earthly body, my mind immediately began receiving divine impartation. My knowledge was perfected. All types of information flooded my brain at an incredible rate of speed. Things were sorting through my brain at lightning speed. I had an awareness of answers to questions that had plagued me for years. Imagine having all of your questions answered in an instant. A dark curtain had been lifted from my understanding. Everything made sense now. There were no missing pieces to the "puzzles of life." It was so exhilarating. My consciousness was experiencing a myriad of sights and sounds.

The majesty of space unfolded to me as I saw it for the first time through the eyes of the Creator. I had never felt so alive, and yet so totally at peace. While I was in Jesus' arms, I was not afraid of anything. Being with Jesus is the safest place in the universe! And I was learning about God from God Himself. I could feel love radiating from Him to me. It was amazing to me that He was so big and powerful, yet deeply concerned about my feelings.

As we continued on our journey, before us, dazzling in a brilliance that pierced the blackness of space, was a star shining across the dark void. It seemed as if I was looking directly into the sun. It was absolutely beautiful. It was white with yellowish gasses floating in an orbit-like movement around it. The scene was brilliant! It probably would have been blinding to the human eye, but I was looking at it with my spiritual eyes. I learned many things about God that day. This was His creation. I had to realize that it was God's nature to create, and

His creation praises and adores Him. The Bible records that the trees and rocks will praise Him. I understood more about God's ability to create and the affect He has on His own creation. Wherever He manifests, new life is born. If He walked through the desert, it would bloom and bud with flowers. Water would gush from rocks, and animals would feed and flourish there. God's presence engenders the creation process itself.

Jesus flew me past a star going nova. It was white and brilliant. Blinding white light shot in every direction from the center of the star. The scene looked like satellite images that I had seen in magazines on earth, but now I was observing this marvel in person. I was also surprised by the colors exhibited in deep space. The refraction of light coming from the heavenly bodies was amazing. It was not all white. It contained a beautiful mixture of colors. I saw electric blues, yellows, and deep pinks. It was like the Aurora Borealis on steroids. This same creative power is also at work inside of us. No sickness can stand in His presence unhealed. No death can stand in His presence without being resurrected. He is by nature the Prince of Life and the Creator of all we know.

I marveled at how incredibly fast the Lord and I were flying through space, my spirit being carried by the Spirit of Jesus Himself. Even as we flew I had never felt so loved. I knew Jesus loved me more than anyone else ever could. Father God accompanied us, and His Spirit seemed to fill all of space above us. I was aware of His presence, but I never did see His face. There seemed to be a smoke or a cloud covering Him. I am sure that He wanted to protect me. I was not afraid because the love of God dispelled all my fears.

Suddenly, emerging from the blackness of space, something was taking shape in front of me. A small, glowing ball became visible. As we got closer, it grew in size. At first it was a small point of light. The light grew and grew, and I saw it directly in front of us, like a planet. All of a sudden we were there—Heaven, my home. It loomed large in front of us. Jesus let me know immediately that I was not going to be allowed to stay. He told me I was only there for a visit.

He flew me over the walls and set me down inside. He put me on a small, grassy hill just inside the walls. He told me that I was forbidden to enter the city by one of the gates because it was not my time to die yet. He said people entered through the gates only after their deaths. He taught me many things about natural and spiritual laws including that it would have been unlawful or what I call "spiritually illegal" for me to enter through the gates of the city. If I had walked through the gates I would have physically died on earth. I believe no one would have been able to awaken me. They would have found me not breathing, lying face down on my bed.

THE HEAVENLY REALM

As soon as I arrived, I assessed the atmosphere. I was experiencing the heavenly realm. There was a sense of peace that was indescribable. I was changed, and my body was completely at peace. My spirit, soul, and mind were at peace. I was entirely happy. What a wonderful place! Angels dressed in white robes down to their feet took me on a tour. These angels did not have wings. There were angels without wings, angels with two wings called cherubim, and angels with six wings called seraphim. There are other creatures in Heaven as well. We would call them beasts. They are not frightening, but different from what we consider to be normal. Some of them are part animal and part human. One beast looked like a muscular man, but when he turned around, he had the face of a lion. There were creatures with the body of a lion and the head and wings of an eagle. Many of the creatures are combinations of both men and beasts.

My spirit, soul, and mind were at peace. I was entirely happy!

I was flown over the walls to the outside of the city where I stood on a grassy area looking toward the city. I saw an amber jewel the size of a football imbedded in one section of the wall. It was rounded on each end. I stooped down to approximately one foot off the ground to look closely at the amber stone. I discovered I could look directly through it into the city. It acted as a huge, bejeweled window. The jewels were cut as if a master jeweler hand-cut and inlaid them into the walls. They were absolutely flawless. The jewels were different sizes, but many of them were very large. Because the jewels were transparent, the light of the city spilled through them creating rainbow-colored light on the outside of the walls. The multicolored light cascaded to the ground. The jewels continued to shine on grassy areas leading up to the city walls. The light spilling through the jewels became rainbow pathways of iridescent splendor. The pathways guided people into the city. Their designated pathways were their own particular "birthstone" color. I do not understand the significance of this, only that God has a divine plan for each life.

I was taken back inside the city for a guided tour. I saw beautiful mountains and hills. Heaven is huge and part of it is countryside. I walked directly down Main Street inside the city. Jesus left me after I was safely inside, and an angel continued to escort me throughout the city. The street that led directly down the middle of the city was perfectly straight with intersecting streets at absolutely perfect right and left angles. One thing was apparent to me. I knew the Master Carpenter Himself designed the city. The squares were perfectly square, and the circles were perfectly round. When I stepped onto the street I was barefoot. My foot peeked out from under my flowing white robe and landed on the pavement. As I stepped onto the street, it looked as if I were standing in about four inches of water. The street emitted the most beautiful glow. It reflected as if I was stepping onto a golden mirror. The street looked like water, and I quickly pulled my foot back under my robe. It was a reflex reaction. I "tested" the street again, but when I stepped on it, it was perfectly solid. It was so transparent it looked wet, but it was dry. Then I was strolling down the golden street barefooted.

I walked to the end of the street where there was a small water fountain. The jet sprays were perfectly angled, and the water spouted up in perfect uniformity. As I traveled along the street, I found myself in a setting that closely resembled a little Spanish town. The buildings looked like adobes—simple and elegant. The street wrapped gently around the water fountain in a sort of town square. It was a peaceful, charming area. Millions of people lived in the city. I saw all types of people, young and old. There were all types of nationalities.

Babies were there who had died in infancy and there were aborted babies there who were completely happy and free. The children forgive their parents, and they want their parents to forgive themselves. The children would be hurt to know that their parents and grandparents carry guilt all of their lives. In Heaven, all the children are extremely warm and loving. The children I saw were full of fun with the inquisitiveness of children, yet they had the knowledge of the Kingdom packed inside their little brains. They could have argued down Socrates on his best day. They were full of the knowledge and insight of the adults in the Kingdom. I met six-year-olds with superior intellect who still wanted to sit on my lap.

God allowed me to see a curious sight. There was a baby boy walking around. He looked like he was about four or five months old at his death. He had full, intelligent thinking capacity and was able to talk. He was very small—a little over a foot tall, but he was able to walk. I also saw an elderly couple who had been married on earth. They were Christians who were now happy residents of the city. The baby boy walked up to the older woman and jumped up into her arms. She and her companion cuddled and loved the baby. The child patiently and eagerly received the love of the couple. When they were finished cuddling the baby, he jumped down out of the granny's arms. The little boy went on his way praising God. I had never seen or heard of anything like it on earth. It was an amazing spectacle! The Lord's Words in the Bible rang in my ears, *"Let the children alone, and do not hinder them from coming to Me; for the kingdom of heaven belongs to such as these"* (Matt. 19:14). It was comforting to see how much love the little ones receive in the Kingdom where there is no death, no sickness, and no sadness.

REJOICING AND PRAISING

I went to another section of the city. It was full of people. There was some sort of block party going on. People were dancing and singing in the streets. All of the merriment was focused on God. People would turn toward the direction of God's throne and sing and shout praises to Him. Every bit of rejoicing was directed toward the Lord. There was happiness everywhere. Hurt feelings and sin were nowhere to be found. I noticed the people were in colorful clothing. Heaven was full of color and diversity including the people and their clothing. They wore beautiful, sparkling clothes, as well as dazzling, white robes. They were not dancing the same dances you may see on earth. They were twirling, jumping, and praising God. All of the activities were expressions of praise. The people were excited and so grateful to be there.

Being in Heaven taught me many things about praise. The methods of praising God were expressed in infinite varieties throughout the Kingdom. The city became very quiet when someone was offering a song or poem to the Lord. After the individual finished with the praise, the whole city erupted with excitement as people, angels, and beasts joined in to praise God all together. It was like a mass Hallelujah chorus. God received glory from everything around Him. When someone sculpted a great work of art—God received the praise. If someone painted a lovely picture—God received the glory, because the people knew their talents and abilities were originally given to them by God. God was proud of each and every one of them. Any attempt in Heaven to create something wonderful for others to enjoy blessed the heart of God Himself.

The music in Heaven was incredible! What a wonderful way to express praise to the Father. The music had great diversity. Some refrains were lilting. The melodies were intriguing and their magnetic refrains played over and over in my spirit. The words were meaningful. They spoke of honor, covenant, majesty, goodness, mercy, and truth. Although they sang, shouted, and talked with their voices, people often communicated non-verbally, like telepathically. And the language barriers were gone. Every culture and nationality understood each other. When the Father or Jesus communicated with me, sometimes it was through verbal language, and other times it was telepathically. We can hear God and others thinking to one another. There are no secrets in Heaven. We do not hear every thought people are thinking, but we can hear other's thoughts in our heads if they are close in proximity, as if someone was speaking directly to us.

I could never have imagined such a place. Every detail was precise. It was not just a place of purpose. It was a land of righteousness and beauty. It is a Kingdom based on fulfilled covenants. It is a land of unbroken promises. Christians have told me they think Heaven is a sort of dreamy-like state. It is just the opposite—it is the ultimate reality. Everything was so real!

—————— ⚬⁄◊ ——————

Christians have told me they think Heaven is a sort of dreamy-like state. It is just the opposite— it is the ultimate reality.

—————— ⚬⁄◊ ——————

The angels of God continued to escort me throughout the city. As I walked along a glowing golden street, I looked to the left over a small, grassy knoll, and I saw Jesus walking along the street parallel to me. He was with an entourage of several other men. Some of them were angels who appeared like men dressed in white. The angels did not have wings. Some of the group was comprised of people. It was hard to tell who was a person and who was an angel. They looked identical except for their faces. Angelic faces seem to be more round than human faces. The humans' faces were also distinctive because they denoted a particular age. Angels have an "ageless" quality.

His Glory

The Bible tells us the Lamb, or Jesus, is the light of the city. The Bible records that, *"...the city has no need of the sun or of the moon to shine on it, for the glory of God has illumined it, and its lamp is the Lamb"* (Rev. 21:23). When Jesus first appeared to me, He came in response to my call for help. He came as Jesus the Savior and lover of my soul. Now as I saw Him in Heaven on the golden street, He was engulfed in an orb of glorious white light. His countenance glowed like our sun, only brighter. The light that was emanating from Jesus was the whitest, brightest light that anyone could imagine. His light was like electric splendor. There was no color variation in His glow. It was pure white in color. The light formed a circle approximately four feet in diameter around Him. The light was the glory and anointing of God. When He walked down the street, it was as if the sun fell from the sky and was slowly moving along the ground with Him. Jesus was a self-generating ball of fire. If one were to look directly into the middle of the fireball, he would see the form of a man walking in its center. It would be Jesus. Light shone from every fiber of His being.

Another time while strolling along the street accompanied by the angels, we were walking behind a hill. I saw what I thought was the sun beginning to rise. I soon discovered I was not witnessing the dawn of a new day when Jesus Himself came walking over the hill toward me. Jesus told me something then that He wants me to share with the people of the earth. Jesus wants us to get close to Him. He wants us to feel His glory and anointing. He wants to pull us into the inner circle of His presence. He wants to see our faces bathed in the glorious light of the anointing of God. He wants us to walk with Him inside the orb of fire of His glory.

My heavenly experiences gave me a whole new perspective of the phrases "Kingdom living" and being "a child of the King." When I stood in the heavenly realm, I realized that this wonderful place had a King. It had royal subjects, and I was one of them. Earth has her kings and Heaven has its King of kings and Lord of lords. There were laws governing the land. They are heavenly laws, which are being taught to its inhabitants by the Holy Spirit. There were seasons and times for various forms of pageantry. Saints are commended for their loyalty to the Lord while they were here on earth.

Words of peace and gratitude were spoken to them by none other than God Himself. God said things like, "Well done. I particularly liked how you handled that situation. When people were hateful to you at work, you baked cookies for them and showed them love. You were faithful to Me, and I appreciated your efforts." How would you like to be given praise from the King of the Universe for baking cookies? There were degrees of rewards in Heaven. There was a lot of pageantry and ceremony in Heaven. There were ceremonies when deceased Christians got their crowns. They were rewarded according to their service on earth just as a military person received a medal for valor or heroism.

There were crowns on saints' heads that were soul winner's crowns. Upon closer examination of a crown, there were many stars on it. They actually looked like thousands of points of light. I stared down through the brightness at all the sparkles. To my amazement, I realized the stars in the crowns were bits of real stars like the stars in the sky. They were unevenly cut as if God pulled them apart and fit them into the crowns with His own fingers. They were small fragments of planetary material, which gave off pure light and energy. The stars were being held in place by some sort of invisible force field. It was a dazzling display when the saints turned to the left and right displaying their crowns, shafts of light shone from each pinpoint of star. I have never seen anything on earth equal to it! The light rays were so bright they would have blinded the natural eye.

There was a great deal of light everywhere in the city. It was the glory and anointing of God. I was keenly aware of the fact that I was in a Kingdom with the real and living God. Every song, every poem, every dance was directed toward God, Jesus, and the Holy Spirit. They were all expressions of the love of the people and heavenly creatures for their God. The music was like the song of a siren; captivating to the soul. When the heavenly choir began to sing, everyone froze. The songs were so beautiful that no one wanted to miss a word or a note being sung. I am still curious about how the singers sang as high as they did. They hit notes that reached octaves above the highest pitches sung on earth. I enjoyed the diversity of the heavenly choirs. Some choirs were made up of Christians. Some choirs were comprised of angels only. Some were mixed with humans, angels, and other creatures all praising and adoring God. Talk about variety. The sights and sounds of the celestial city were magnificent!

RETURNING HOME

At last it was time for me to return home from my heavenly visit. Jesus scooped me up in His loving arms and flew me back up over the wall. My heart pounded with the excitement of the descent. It must be like the sensation astronauts feel while descending into the earth's atmosphere. I felt like I was quickly falling a great distance at an incredible rate of speed. We descended down through the atmosphere just the way we had ascended.

The closer I got to earth, the less I remembered. The sensation I got as I flew up to Heaven reversed itself. I could not remember the answers to the questions that had been bothering me for years. I remember praying, "God, please don't take the knowledge of Heaven away from me," but it was as if God did not hear me. My mind started to cloud up like a veil was being dropped on it. Unanswered questions stuck in my mind. The glory of Heaven was closing to me. God gently told me it would be unlawful for me to remember everything I had seen and known.

As Jesus and I descended through the atmosphere the moon was on our right. I saw the stars and planets. I could see the roof of my home and my body lying face down on the bed. As soon as Jesus deposited my spirit back into my body, I experienced a jolting sensation. It felt like I was in a skyscraper elevator and had just descended many floors in a few seconds. I was a little dizzy at first. I took a huge breath. I had to breathe deeply to fill my lungs with air. I do not know how many hours I was lying face down in the suspended state. As soon as my spirit reentered my body, it was like being awakened abruptly from a deep sleep.

I could not end this story without saying that you do not want to miss God's Heaven. There is beauty and majesty awaiting all who have placed their trust in God through Jesus. He has laid up crowns for us and robes of splendor. There are loved ones and great men and women from the pages of history to meet. God's Kingdom is not magical or mystical. It is real. The great message of the Bible is that Jesus paid the price to enable us to approach God in His holiness in Heaven. I have the assurance that if I died tonight, I would go to be with Jesus in all His holy glory in Heaven forever. He is offering you the same opportunity to come to this assurance.

Commentary

Why Jesus chooses some people to take to Heaven is a mystery, but we are told of realms most of us have never experienced or ever imagined. Jubilee's story began when she cried out to Jesus to rescue her from despair, and He was immediately at her side. As Lord of the galaxies and firmaments, Jesus easily flew her through them and then took her to the City of God in Heaven. What Jubilee saw and experienced dispels any limited views of what our personal eternity will be like. The expanse, the beauty and the creativity, the myriad of different types of angelic and other beings, the sounds of worship that permeate the atmosphere, the presence of God Himself, all far exceed our loftiest expectations. Every being in Heaven is filled with the glory, the joy, the personal love of God to the fullest—and His rewards to us for the loving choices we have made while on earth are plentiful. One day every question you've ever had about the Lord will be fully answered when you see Him as He is, in all of His glory, on the day you walk through those gates of Heaven.

About Jubilee Mitchell

Jubilee began receiving prophetic dreams/visions at a young age. She retired early from civil service, working with the U.S. Air Force, and became founder and CEO of IIRRAD—Individuals in River Research and Development. She now spreads the gospel of Jesus as an evangelist and serves as volunteer staff at Life Church in Fenton, Missouri, where she also "signs" the services for the deaf. She is the author of *Journey of Comfort* and is working on two other books.

CHAPTER 3

LIVING TESTIMONY TO THE RESURRECTION

by Ian McCormack

Despite the fact that Ian, a New Zealander, was an experienced night diver, surfing and fishing with the local Creole divers in the earthly paradise island of Mauritius in the Indian Ocean, this night he felt uneasy about going out. Nevertheless, he let himself be persuaded and went anyway.

As I dived that night, the beam of my torch light picked out a jellyfish right in front of me. I was fascinated because of its shape. Not until I squeezed it through my leather-gloved hand did I realize that this was a box jellyfish, or sea wasp—the second deadliest creature known to humankind. Its toxin had killed more than seventy Australians; and up in the northern parts of Australia, it had killed more people than had been killed by sharks. The sting from this fish stopped the heart of a 38-year-old man in ten minutes.

Suddenly, I experienced what felt like a huge electric shock in my forearm, like thousands of volts of electricity. Not being able to see what had happened, I did the worst thing possible. I rubbed my arm, and so rubbed in the poison from the tentacles of the jellyfish. Before I could get out onto the reef, another box jellyfish stung me. My forearm was swollen like a balloon. Where the tentacles had stung were burn-like blisters across my arm, and I felt on fire as the poison began moving round in my body. It hit my lymph glands as if I had been punched, and my breathing quickly became constricted. I knew I needed hospitalization and quickly! I began to shake violently. Then a deadly cold crept over my entire body right to my bone marrow. I could feel a darkness creeping over the inner part of my bones. Death was creeping over me.

I knew my body was dying right before my eyes. Somehow I got to shore. I was incredibly cold. Lying on my back and feeling the poison taking its effect, I heard a quiet voice saying, "Son, if you close your eyes you will never wake again." I had no idea that it was the Lord who had said it until much later; but being a qualified lifeguard and instructor in scuba, I knew that unless I was given an antitoxin quickly, I would die.

Someone called for an ambulance. During the journey to the hospital, my life flashed before me and I thought, *I'm going to die.* This is what happens before you die, your life is displayed before you. Despite being an atheist, I did wonder whether there was any life after death. Then my mother's face came before me and said, "Ian, no matter how far from God you are, if you will cry out to God from your heart, God will hear you, and God will forgive you." Having traveled throughout Southeast Asia and seen a million gods, I thought to myself, *Pray to God? Which one?* But, my mother's face was still there, and she had only ever prayed to the Christian God.

I thank God for my praying mother who had not given up on a stubborn, rebellious son.

It had been ten years since I had spoken to my mother about God, ten years of total denial that God existed, yet my mother was still praying for me. Later, when I returned to New Zealand, I compared notes with her. God had shown her my face and said to her that night, "Your son is nearly dead. Start now, and pray for him." I thank God for my praying mother who had not given up on a stubborn, rebellious son.

I remembered that my mother had taught me the Lord's Prayer, though I could just barely recall it. My mind went almost completely blank, but I could hear my mother saying, "From your heart, son, pray from your heart." A prayer then came from my heart, "God, if You're real and this prayer is real, help me remember the prayer my mother taught me. If there is anything soft or good left in my heart, please help me to remember the Lord's Prayer." Before my eyes the words appeared, "Forgive us our sins." I knew this meant I had to ask God to forgive all the sins I had ever committed; but I told God that I felt like a hypocrite, praying on my deathbed. But if He could possibly forgive me, then I was sincere in crying out to Him to forgive my sins. It seemed as though God had heard, for another part of the prayer came up, "Forgive those who have sinned against you."

One verse after another of the Lord's Prayer came to my mind as I responded to each one from my heart to the Lord. When I got to "Thy will be done on earth as it is in Heaven," I thought, *Your will? God's will?* I had been doing my own thing for twenty-four years! I promised God, however, that if I came through this experience alive, I would find out what was His will for me, and follow Him all the days of my life. As I prayed that prayer, I knew I had made peace with God. Almost immediately the ambulance doors opened. I was lifted into a wheelchair and raced into the hospital where the doctors administered the antitoxin.

I was conscious of the fact that if I drifted out of my body it would mean death. I knew this was no weird trip or hallucination; this was real. I was also aware that I could not feel my arms at all, and I could no longer keep my eyes open. I remember closing my eyes and breathing a sigh of relief. At that point, from what I ascertained from the hospital, I died and was pronounced clinically dead.

The scariest thing was the moment my eyes closed, I was suddenly wide awake again, standing by what I thought was my bed in pitch black darkness. It was so dark I could not even see my hand in front of my face. I lifted my right hand up to touch my face, it seemed either to miss it, or go straight through. I put both hands up to touch my face and they seemed to pass straight through it. That was the strangest feeling. What followed was even worse, because I realized I could not touch any part of my physical form. Yet I had the sensation of being a complete human being with all my faculties—yet I did not have a flesh and bone form.

My next thought was, *Where on earth am I?* because I could feel the most intense evil pervading the darkness surrounding me. It was as if the darkness took on a spiritual dimension. There was a totally evil spiritual presence that started to move toward me. Although I still could not see, I sensed something looking at me out of the darkness. Then to my right came a voice that yelled, "Shut up!" as if it could hear my thoughts. As I backed off from the voice, another one from the left shouted,

"You deserve to be here!" My arms came up to protect myself and I asked, "Where am I?" A third voice replied, "You're in hell, now shut up." Some people think hell is just a big party, but I tell you it's going to be pretty hard to grab your beer down there when you can't even find your face!

I stood there in that blackness long enough to put the fear of God into me for eternity. But at the moment of deepest blackness, a brilliant light shone upon me and drew me straight out. It was not like walking, but being translated up in a supernatural way. As I was drawn up into the light, it seemed to touch my face and encase my entire being, as if it had pierced into the deepest darkness and pulled me out. God told me later that if I had not prayed that death-bed prayer in the ambulance, I would have stayed in hell. Thank God for His grace and mercy that hears a sinner's prayer even in the last seconds of his life—though I do not recommend taking the risk of waiting that long.

Looking back, I was able to see the darkness fading on either side, and could feel the power and presence of this light drawing me up into a circular opening far above me, like a speck of dust caught up in a brilliant beam of sunlight.

TUNNEL OF LIGHT

Almost immediately, I entered the opening and, looking down the tunnel, I could see the source of the light. The radiance, the power and purity that was flowing from it was awesome. As I looked, a wave of thicker, intense light broke away from the source, and came down the tunnel at incredible speed as if to greet me. A wave of warmth and comfort actually went through my entire being, and I felt the most incredible, soothing feeling I have ever experienced.

About half way down the tunnel, another wave of light broke off and came toward me. When it touched me, I felt the most wonderful peace go right through me, in exactly the same way as before. This was total peace. In my past, I had sought peace in education, sports, travel, in almost every avenue possible, yet it had eluded me. This, however, was a living peace that seemed to remain as this light left its deposit within me.

Previously, in the darkness, I could see nothing. But now, in the light, to my amazement, I saw my hand was like a spirit form, full of white radiant light, the same light that was coming from the end of the tunnel. I wanted to go; and as I began to move, another wave of light came, pure joy and excitement enveloped me.

It looked like a white fire, or a mountain of cut diamonds sparkling with the most indescribable brilliance.

What I saw next blew my mind. It looked like a white fire, or a mountain of cut diamonds sparkling with the most indescribable brilliance. And yet, as I stopped at the end of this tunnel of light, to the left, right, and above me, everywhere seemed totally filled with this iridescent light, reaching to the extremity of my vision, out into infinity. I wondered for a moment if there was a person in the center of this brilliance, or whether it was just a force of good or power in the universe.

A voice came out of the light and said, "Ian, do you wish to return?" I could not work it out for the moment. *Return where?* I thought. But as I looked back over my shoulder and saw the tunnel going back into darkness and thought of the hospital bed, I realized I did not know where I was and the words came from me, "I wish to return." The voice responded, "Ian, if you wish to return, you must see in a new light." The moment I heard those words, "See in a new light," words appeared before me: *"God is Light, and in Him there is no darkness at all"* (1 John 1:5). They were words on a Christmas card given to me in South Africa, but I had not known that they were taken from the New Testament.

As I saw these words in front of me, I realized the light could be coming from God, and, if it was, then what was I doing here? They must have made a mistake because I did not deserve to be here. *If He knows my name, and He knows my thoughts as speech, then I am transparent before Him,* I thought. *He can see everything I've ever done in my life.* In fear I thought, *I'm getting out of here.* I started pulling back, looking for some rock to crawl under, or go back down the tunnel where I thought I belonged. But as I pulled back from His presence, wave after wave of pure light started flooding upon me.

The first wave that touched me caused my hands and body to tingle as I felt love go into the depths of who I was, to the extent that I staggered. Then another wave came, and yet another. I thought, *God, You can't love me, I've committed so many sins, I've cursed You, I've broken so many commandments.* The waves of love kept coming to me, and every statement I confessed was followed by another wave of love until I stood there weeping as God's love washed through me again and again. I could not believe that God could love such a filthy, unclean man. Yet, as I stood in His presence, the love got stronger and stronger until I felt that if only I could step into the light and see Him, I would know who God was.

I walked closer and closer, until suddenly the light opened up and I saw the bare feet of a Man with dazzling white garments around His ankles. As I looked up, it seemed as if the light emanated from the pores of His entire face, like brilliant jewels with light and power shooting out from every facet. In total wonder at the sight of the brilliance and purity before me, I realized this person indeed must be God. It could only be Jesus. His garments appeared to be made of shimmering light itself. I walked up closer to see His eyes, but as I stood in front of Him, He moved away as if He did not want that. And as He moved, I saw what looked like a brand-new planet Earth opening up before me.

This new earth had green grass, yet with the same light and radiance that was upon God. Through the fields, a crystal clear river flowed, with trees on either side of its banks. There were green rolling hills, mountains and blue skies over to my right; and to my left, meadows with flowers and trees. It looked like a Garden of Eden or paradise. Every part of me was drinking this in saying, "I belong here. I was made for this place. I've traveled the world looking for a place like this." I wanted to enter in and explore, but as I stepped forward to do so, He stepped in front of me and asked me this question, "Ian, now that you have seen, do you wish to step in, or return?"

Imagine if you had gotten there, as it were, by the skin of your teeth, through a deathbed prayer.

Imagine if you knew that, just behind God, was a place where there would be no more sickness, no more death, no more suffering, no more pain, no more wars, and where there was life for eternity, what would you do? Believe me, I had no plans to come back to this earth. I was going to say goodbye to this cruel world and step right into that one.

But that instant I looked back over my shoulder. I saw a clear vision of my mother looking at me. She had prayed for me every day of my life, and had tried to show me the way of God. I realized that if I went into Heaven right then she would think I had gone to hell, because she would not know of my repentance in that ambulance and giving my life to God. I said, "God, I can't step in, I can't be selfish. I must go back and tell my mother that what she believes in is real."

I must go back and tell my mother that what she believes in is real.

Looking back, I saw all my family and thousands upon thousands of people stretching far back into the distance. I asked God who they were, and He said that if I did not return, many of those people would most likely never hear about Him. My response was that I did not love them; but as I expressed that feeling, God said, "But I do, and I want them to come to know Me."

How was I to get back? God told me to tilt my head, feel liquid running from my eye, and then open it and see. I found myself with my right eye open, and there was a doctor at the end of the bed with a sharp instrument prodding my foot. As he turned and saw me, the blood drained from his face, and you could see him thinking, *A corpse has just opened its eye.*

I heard the voice of God whisper, "Son, I've just given you your life back."

Still trying to grasp what I had seen, I heard the voice of God whisper, "Son, I've just given you your life back." My response to God, "If that is true, could You please give me strength to turn my head and look through my other eye?" As God gave me strength to open my left eye, I saw in the doorway of the room, nurses and orderlies. They were standing in the doorway staring, open-mouthed. I had been dead for fifteen minutes; but now I was very much alive!

I tried to move my neck. I thought that if I had been dead that long, I could be a quadriplegic for the rest of my life. So I asked God to heal me completely, and allow me to walk out of the hospital, otherwise to take me back into Heaven. Over the next four hours, I felt warmth and power flow through my body—the next day I walked out of the hospital, completely healed.

Over the next six weeks I read the Bible from Genesis to Revelation. As I read through the Scriptures, everything that I had seen in Heaven was described in that book. I believe Jesus the Messiah died for our sins on the cross, rose from the dead, and is the Resurrection and the Life.

I believe in resurrection power.

I believe in healing.

I am a living testimony to it all.

Commentary

The Lord does warn even those who do not believe in Him when trouble is ahead; but like Ian, many do not heed the warnings. Ian's sense of uneasiness was a warning he didn't heed. The gracious mercy of the Lord and a praying mother enabled Ian to hear the Lord's voice speaking to him to keep his eyes open. Even the feeble prayer Ian prayed was enough to rescue him from an eternity in the darkness of hell. The Bible tells us, *"But your iniquities have made a separation between you and your God, and your sins have hidden His face from you..."* (Isa. 59:2). Ian, an atheist, had been so far from the Lord that when He saw Jesus in all His light, he had no recognition of Him such as someone who knows the Lord immediately has. Then he surmised He must be God.

As the Lord begins to show Ian His love, Ian wanted to flee from Him back into darkness as he saw his own unworthiness. But the love of the Lord overcame Ian's feelings of uncleanness in His presence until he then wanted to come closer to Him, to know who He was.

That shift in the spirit realm, where Ian realized his sin before God and then received His forgiveness, wanting to draw near to him, he experienced being "born again" of the Spirit of God.

When anyone has a "born again" experience, we become new persons who are now responsive to the Spirit of God who comes to dwell within us. Little by little, God works in our lives to make us righteous as He is righteous. We can see that process already beginning in Ian's life. Despite living a self-indulgent life, when Ian is given the choice of staying in Heaven or going back to earth, he realizes his mother would think he had gone to hell and never know he was in Heaven if he didn't go back. The unselfishness of this choice reveals that a change was already beginning to happen in Ian.

One of the things that takes place when we are born again is that we begin to change and become more loving and more forgiving, all of which is to say, more like Jesus in increasing measure. Ian now cared more about his mother than even his own preference to stay in Heaven. The Lord told Ian that many thousands of people would never know about Him and His offer of forgiveness and the way to Heaven if Ian did not return to earth. Ian responded that he didn't really care about them. But Jesus replied that He loved them. Here too is another remarkable thing about being born again. Jesus begins to give us His love for others, even those whom we might never have cared about before. God has no favorites. He loves us all equally.

> *For God so loved the* [whole] *world* [and every-one in it] *that He gave His only begotten Son that whoever believes in Him shall not perish, but have eternal life* (John 3:16).

About Ian McCormack

Born and raised in New Zealand, following his life-after-death experience in 1982, Ian has traveled the world sharing his experience in more than fifty-five nations. He is an ordained minister with the New Zealand Assemblies of God and is currently the pastor at Kingsgate Church in London, England. His heart is to see many souls come to know the Lord as their personal Savior. The following story is Ian's son Michael's testimony of also being in Heaven with Jesus.

CHAPTER 4

THE BEAUTIFUL PLACE

by Michael McCormack

Michael is the son of Ian McCormack whose story you just read. Michael was ten years old when he had this encounter with Jesus in Heaven in a vision. The McCormack's live in London, England. Try reading this with Michael's delightful British accent telling the story.

When I came into church, I felt led to sit down and pray to Jesus. As I did, a light shone on me and with that light came an overflowing love. I was then lifted up into the heavens in this white light. I saw angels coming around me, surrounding me as I went up. They were clothed in white robes and had shining faces and wings. They were floating around me, like they were hovering.

Their wings were fully open and moving quite slowly— and they were barefooted.

Then I arrived at Heaven's Gate. It was golden. Beyond the gate I could see a massive palace and a town. The palace and the town were surrounded by a wall, which was also golden in color. Jesus was suddenly next to me in white shining clothing. I saw the shape of His face that was all light, so it was hard to see His face clearly, but I was aware that He had very kind eyes. He was tall. I felt surprised, happy, and amazed all at the same time. Jesus didn't speak to me then, but I heard God the Father's voice say to me from inside the city, "Come, My son." When He said it, I saw the massive golden gate open toward me by itself; and I saw a bright shining light coming out as the gate opened.

WALKING WITH JESUS

Jesus took me through lovely meadows in which I saw animals such as rabbits, deer, and foxes. Then I walked with Jesus as He took me to the Throne Room of God. It had sparkling lights and golden pillars and paintings like seen in old churches—and there were jewels everywhere in the room. I saw two rows of angels with banners on the end of golden trumpets. The banners were purple and golden with no picture on them. The trumpets were long like they have in C.S. Lewis' story of Narnia when they crowned Edmond, Peter, Susan, and Lucy. There were big angels with white robes and wings coming out of their backs, but their wings were all folded down. They had faces like men, happy faces and very bright, but not as bright as Jesus.

My knees were shaking because I was so overwhelmed at all of what I was seeing. I was also crying and jumping up and down. There was the noise of the trumpeting and a lot of background sounds and the angels were singing "Hosanna" and other songs I did not recognize. They were playing with harps and some things that looked like tambourines, small drums with small cymbals. There were creatures around the throne that were not like animals on earth, but rather combinations of different animals, such as a lion with eagle's wings coming out of its lion-like back. But they were not scary.

Then Jesus held out a staff in His hand. It was wooden like a shepherd's staff. I looked to where it was pointed and I saw three thrones. As I looked at each one, they somehow looked like they were joined together, as if they were one throne. Just as the Father, Son, and Holy Spirit are all one God, so these thrones were three yet one. It is sometimes hard to describe things like that in our world. The thrones were golden, and I saw jewels covering the thrones. The jewels were all the colors of the rainbow and more. I saw emeralds, rubies, blue sapphires, yellow stones and purple ones, plus ones I had never seen before.

―――――― ⌒〜⌒ ――――――

I was taken up into these clouds and began to dance with the angels.

―――――― ⌒〜⌒ ――――――

I looked up and saw no roof above the throne. I saw clouds above the throne like the Northern Lights but much brighter and more colorful. They were dancing colors and angels were dancing in the clouds in a line. I was taken up into these clouds and began to dance with the angels. I felt so joyful, so amazed, and so full of life.

The Tree of Life

Then the Lord took me outside to the town. The town was lined with golden roads. There were many houses, all different. We came to a river, the River of Life. It was crystal clear and fast flowing; and it was coming out from a tree I knew was the Tree of Life. The Tree of Life had loads of fruit on it, and somehow I knew that each day the youngest children came and took a piece of fruit to share it with their families. Everyone in Heaven is part of a big family. They lived on that fruit for the day. There was different varieties of fruit on the tree—pomegranates, apples, grapes, oranges, bananas—every type of fruit was growing on the same tree. The tree was like a big, strong oak tree and it had a thick trunk. And the water was flowing from the Tree of Life into the houses; it was empowering them, giving them light. Jesus cupped His hands together and dipped them into the River of Life. Then He began to pour water over my head, like He was anointing me, and I felt power coming into me.

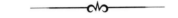

Jesus poured water over my head, and I felt power coming into me.

Then Jesus took me to a door. It was a normal door made from an oak tree. There was a jewel on the end of the knob. It was a ruby. I felt like He wanted me to open the door, so I put my hand on the handle and opened it. I went through the door, which opened into a beautiful garden—the New Earth. As I went into the garden, I saw it was filled with wildlife, lakes, waterfalls, and rainbows. Animals, mostly deer, were drinking from a lake. It was like a rainforest only more colorful and full of life. It smelled lovely and was so wonderful and beautiful. Jesus spoke to me, "This is the New Earth that we will treasure."

Then Jesus took me out into space and showed me the old earth. It was like seeing a satellite picture of Earth from space. It was grey and dull and covered and surrounded by a black mist, and the mist was sin. He seemed sad, and I felt His sadness inside my heart. The

Lord then took me down to visit it, and all the buildings were crumbled and destroyed. There was no life in it at all. All the plants had died. I saw no people—it was deserted.

Jesus said to me in the same kind voice as before, "This is the earth that man has destroyed." Then He said, "What I have shown you I want more people to see. I have shown you this because I want you to tell the people that you have seen this and that they should turn back to God. This is what is going to happen and you can't stop this…but you can help save more people."

Then Jesus left, and I woke up back in my seat in the church.

Commentary

Jane McCormack, Michael's mother, had this to say about Michael's experience. "This is every parents' dream that the Lord would take their children and show them His heavenly Kingdom. We know our son, and this is a totally genuine experience. It was incredible to see this happen to him; but at times during the encounter it was somewhat fearful as I could see the fear and awe of the Lord upon Michael's little face as I watched him. We feel that the Lord commissioned Michael that very night before our eyes." When I (Lonnie) interviewed Michael by telephone, he told me, "I feel it's my mission to tell people. So I'm not worried when I have to speak in front of a whole church. The Holy Spirit often comes upon the people when I do." This is a young man who is assured of his calling in God. When I asked what impact it had on him to see the world destroyed by sin, Michael said, "I know I won't be there. I'm going to that beautiful place, so there's nothing to fear." We would all do well to adopt Michael's attitude and assurance and fully put our treasure in Heaven.

But according to His promise we are looking for new heavens and a new earth, in which righteousness dwells (2 Peter 3:13).

About Michael McCormack
(written by his father)

Born in New Zealand, Michael is a most amazing young boy. He has a heart of gold and is a very caring and loving young man. His passion is for all types of sports, fishing, and diving. He has lived in about fifteen different nations and is currently attending a Christian school in London, England. He has two sisters, Lisa and Sarah. His grandparents live in New Zealand and Canada.

The Lord has really begun to open the heavens above Michael's life, and it is astounding to hear all the Lord continues to reveal to him.

CHAPTER 5

A PALESTINIAN IS TAKEN TO HEAVEN

by Khalida Wukawitz

Born in Palestinian Bethlehem, Khalida was orphaned at a young age and sold as a slave child to a Muslim Bedouin tribe. There she learned the Qur'an and also about Jihad. Walking for years barefooted with her personal camel as they traveled in caravan back and forth throughout the Arab nations, she was eventually married off to a Muslim man who abused her and then took her daughter and abandoned her. She was married off again and brought to the United States, but kept in isolation. When her life was threatened by her husband's beatings, she managed to flee with her two children. Homeless and penniless, a Christian woman saw her plight

> *and offered her a job and a home for her and*
> *her children. This is where Khalida's story*
> *picks up.*

A Christian woman I worked for had been sharing her faith with me for two years. I was raised as a Palestinian, and even though I was sure my Islamic faith was the only true faith, I wanted to have peace and love like she did. For two years she told me about Jesus, but because of how I was raised, I couldn't believe God had a Son. After all, I was raised with the Qur'an and I loved Mohammed.

But finally I started asking more questions about her faith. At the same time I was fasting more, and saying more Islamic prayers, asking Allah to show himself to me. I prayed, "If you are the truth, why would you not come to me to show me the truth?"

One day I was at the store, working in the back room. I thought, *Nothing is working. I'm making money, but I'm so unhappy. Where is the truth?* Even though it didn't make sense to me about Him, I said, "Jesus, if You are the Son of God, come down and show me." That moment, something happened in the room. The room itself changed. All of a sudden a person was standing in front of me, but different from any person I'd ever known. I heard His voice—it was the same voice I heard years before. Though I didn't know who it was then, He said over and over to me when my Muslim husband was beating me and threatening my life, "Leave the darkness for the light." He said in Arabic, "I am the truth, the life, and the way, and no one comes to the Father except by Me."

His voice was like rushing waters, powerful and soothing at the same time. The minute He said, "I am the truth," I knew immediately it was Jesus. He didn't say, "I am Jesus," but every fiber of my being knew who He was. I had never read the Bible before, but somehow I knew what Jesus was saying to me was in the Bible. I was so consumed by His presence that I dropped to my knees and looked up at Him. He is so glorious, so beautiful. All light inside of Light. I said, "Lord! You *are* Lord!" He said, "Yes, I am Jesus, the One you denied. The One you said is not the Son of God. I came to save you, to make you a happy person. You don't have to do anything, just know that I love you." I said, "That's it?" He said, "Yes, believe in Me." It was like I went to school and studied everything in one day. All of a sudden Jesus made sense to me.

He started walking closer to me. It took only a split second and Jesus was right there before me. He got so close that there was too much light to even see the color of His eyes. It was not like looking at any human being. Somehow with His being and His voice came light. A huge light. An overwhelming light. As He was with me for a while, I became part of Heaven. The room was so changed it wasn't the room any more. I thought, *I am not on earth anymore.* He was talking to me, but at the same time I was seeing Heaven right before my eyes.

SEEING HEAVEN

Then He said to me, "You are My daughter." The instant the words came out of His mouth, they were like living water. I saw everything in one split second, and I understood as I saw it all happen. He didn't preach to me; He was just talking to me like another person, but with a beautiful and strong voice. It was loving, and sweet like honey. As He got closer, as He was talking to me, it was revealed to me that He is truly the Son of God and that He had died on the cross. I also knew that He is the Lion and the King. It all was revealed to me at once. I also knew that He is a Father and I was His daughter and His chosen one. All the pain in my life He already knew about, and He was already pleased with me. I knew that all is forgiven by the blood of Jesus. All this I knew just being in His presence.

It all was revealed to me at once.

Jesus stood on my right side. I saw three men who were surrounded by light. The one who appeared to be the oldest had a long beard and was wearing a royal robe.

Jesus told me that they were Abraham, Isaac, and Jacob. Jesus introduced them to me without words. He said, "Go to the bosom of your father Abraham." Jesus looked at me and assured me, "Do not be in fear. Go to the bosom of Father Abraham." I then went. I walked to Abraham, and he welcomed me and said, "Come to me, my daughter." He was sitting, and I sat on his lap and rested my head on his shoulder. Jesus told me to repent from the curse words that we used to curse the Jewish people. I spoke in Arabic and asked for forgiveness. Abraham said my repentance was received by the Lord. I said, "I want to see this in my lifetime." As I said that, I saw it written, "On earth as it is in heaven."[1] I was requesting it for the earth, and Jesus affirmed that my request would take place on the earth. I then went back to Jesus.

I began to recognize more things in Heaven. There was no language barrier. I understood angels were saying, "Holy, holy, holy." I saw a huge crown and people threw it at the feet of Jesus. I saw children under the age of six, and they were all worshiping Jesus. Jesus was speaking to me, explaining things to my mind about what I was seeing. These were the babies who died when their mothers got rid of them through abortion. Some died naturally through sickness or were murdered. All of them were at Jesus' feet and so peaceful and so healthy and happy—not one sad face.

There were multitudes of people. I could hear the sounds of Heaven in every language and tongue, and I saw every color of the millions worshiping Jesus as Lord, calling Him, "Holy, Holy Lamb of God" over and over. I saw water, crystal clear water. Everyone was healthy. As I looked at things, I understood them supernaturally. I knew it all by the Spirit of God as I was with them in Heaven dancing before Jesus, dancing around the throne at His feet. He was also the Person who was on the throne.

There is a place by His feet where I saw the angels, the babies, and the birds of the air. It was all so very beautiful. I was worshiping and calling Him "My God, my Savior, and my King." These words were coming out of my mouth. I was still seeing and feeling all this in my body and I was on my knees worshiping Him when Heaven began fading away, though not too quickly. I started sensing that I was back on the earth. I could see Jesus backing away in the room. I was still on my knees though I had been standing when He first spoke to me. I was begging Him not to leave me there. "I need You," I told Him, not wanting to ever be without Him again. He said to me in Arabic, "I'm going to come back and get you," He put His hand on me before He left. Right after that, I was flat on the ground, and I was back in the room and everything of Heaven faded away.

THE SPIRIT OF GOD

I got up and sat on my knees. I began to speak in a language I had heard in Heaven but never on earth. I had never learned about speaking in tongues. I saw the Lion in Heaven, that strong Lion. Now as I spoke in that language, I felt that strength inside of me. All of my life of pain, hurt, and sorrow was suddenly before me. It was as if He took out all the sadness from inside of me and let me see it and then replaced it with everything that is good. I saw so many negative things; they were all before me, but all the good things were there, too. I could see all of it, not only the experiences, but things in my heart as well. I recognized it, and I was able to choose to replace all the bad with the good.

I continued to speak in the heavenly language. I had never used drugs or alcohol in my life, but I had seen people who were drunk—and I was "drunk" with the Spirit of God, something I would read about later that happened to the disciples at Pentecost. I was feeling heavy, yet at the same time as light as if I was dancing on a cloud, like a bird that could fly in the air.

I walked out of the room to the front of the store. I was having a hard time walking, still under the power of the Spirit. I was not scared for one moment. I felt like I had just been with the love of my life. I knew I could trust that Person. I could trust Him entirely. Now I knew who Jesus is. When I walked outside, I saw my dear friend, and I said to her, "I just received Jesus as my personal Savior. I just talked to Jesus. He's my God and my King!" I told her, "He *IS* the way and you do have to believe in Jesus."

He gave me the love, healing, and security that twenty-nine years in the Qur'an never gave me. Now, by a miracle of the Spirit of God, I was quoting many verses from the Bible though I had never read it. I now knew it is not about us and what we do to try and please God, it's all about Jesus and who He is and what He has done for us!

I was filled with the power of Jesus from that day forward. My heart was healed. It was no longer full of hate, anger, confusion, and unforgiveness. I was wholly healed from my childhood as a Palestinian and feeling like a victim of every circumstance. There was such a change in my heart. I wasn't sad anymore. I felt strong, as if I could face life and face any challenges that would come to me now that I had Jesus with me. He gave me freedom and He gave me love.

Commentary

Khalida came from a life that is about as far from faith in Jesus as you can get—she was a slave to a Bedouin tribe, living as a Muslim with no awareness of there being any other faith or any other god than Allah. But God knew exactly where she was, and He sovereignly led her to the Christian woman who took her and her children in and gave them a home when they were homeless. Many times when we come to the Lord we can look back and see that He was there all along in our lives in one way or another, caring for us, protecting us. That certainly was true for Khalida. As she worked for the Christian woman, she remained true to her Islamic faith. Though she maintained her beliefs, it was the love of God that she saw in her Christian friend and employer that Islam did not provide for her. Neither did it provide a relationship with God, one in which He would talk to her as her friend claimed He spoke to her. Allah seemed unresponsive no matter how many Islamic prayers she prayed or how often she fasted.

Finally, out of frustration in wanting to know God, she suddenly called out to Jesus and just as suddenly He was there before her, as if He had been waiting for her to call to Him. He is that close to all of us, waiting to respond to us when we call upon Him with all our hearts, wanting to know Him, or know Him more deeply. He may not come personally to everyone, but that is a prayer He always answers.

What Khalida experienced in Heaven was not something she would ever have imagined as a faithful Muslim, but then, she would not have expected to meet Father Abraham either, or as she would call him in Arabic, Ibrahim. She did as the Lord bid her to do, and asked him for forgiveness for curses she had spoken against the Jewish people. Coming to know Jesus, in Heaven or on the earth, if we are to be His, we must give up our prejudices and exchange what we thought was wrong with others for accepting that we have had wrong attitudes of bitterness, hatred, or pride against others—and ask for forgiveness. As Jesus loves and died for all people so that we all can be forgiven, so must we love and forgive as He does if we are to be His followers. No exceptions allowed!

Never as a Muslim did she ever know the joy of worship and certainly never worship of Jesus whom she had been taught was a prophet of Allah, second to Mohammed. One moment with Jesus and there is complete revelation of who He is. She was calling Him "My God, my Savior, and my King." He is that for all of us who call upon His name.

About Khalida Wukawitz

Khalida's story is probably one of the most unique you'll ever hear. Born in Bethlehem of a Palestinian mother who died days after she was born, she was put in an orphanage that was bombed when she was a little girl. It was never known if the bomb came from the Israelis or the Palestinians. All in the orphanage were killed—except Khalida who was found wandering the streets. She was sold to a Bedouin family where she became their slave. She was given her own camel and was taught the ways of Islam as she walked barefooted and in the same clothes for years as part of a caravan that traveled from one Arab country to the next in search of food. But God's hand was upon her through one difficult situation after another. God sovereignly took her from the sands of an Arab desert to the United States. When she met the Christian woman, she had barely escaped with her children from the husband who had brought her to America but kept her in seclusion. What may look like a very circuitous journey is often a straight path into the arms of Jesus. God was all this time leading her to Himself.

When Khalida met her Christian friend, she spoke very little English. Today she has a college degree and speaks English very well. Khalida's experience of asking Father Abraham to forgive her for cursing the Jewish people had a profound impact on her life. She carries in her heart a desire to see reconciliation between Arabs and Jews and to see Israel honored in the way God has ordained in the Bible. Khalida considers that part of the work God has given her.

The full story of Khalida's life (this is only the barest details) and salvation can be found in *10 Amazing Muslims Touched by God.*[2]

Endnotes

1. See Matthew 6:10.

2. Faisal Malick, *10 Amazing Muslims Touched by God* (Shippensburg, PA: Destiny Image Publishers, 2012).

CHAPTER 6

THE MAGNIFICENCE OF HEAVEN

Dr. Gary Wood

It was two days before Christmas. Gary was listening to his sister softly singing "Silent Night" while he drove the car home that dark night, when suddenly she screamed in horror. A truck was parked illegally on the side of the road and there was no way to avoid hitting it. Gary heard an explosion and felt a sharp searing pain on the lower portion of his face and then, just as suddenly, he was relieved of all pain.

I saw my whole life pass before me in a millisecond in flashes of incidents. There was no confusion about what had just happened. I had nothing but complete peace and tranquility and total absence of pain.

At first, I felt myself at the top of the car, then I was out of it. Then I was caught into a funnel-shaped cloud that kept getting wider and wider. I began to walk on a moving pathway in the cloud—like an airport walkway that enables you to walk more easily. Up, up, up I went; and as I continued, I was engulfed in a brilliant light. Serenity and peace continued to wash over me. As I walked on the pathway, I instinctively knew I was headed north.

Then the swirling mass of a funnel-shaped cloud opened up wide and I saw a giant golden satellite suspended in Heaven. All earthly things are built upon something, but God has this city suspended in Heaven because there's nothing on earth that could hold it. When I approached Heaven, there was an angel with a sword who granted me access into Heaven. Then I was actually standing on the outside of the city, on a lush green carpet of grass on a hill. I started walking up the hill. The grass came all the way through my feet; and when I looked, there were no indentions where I had stepped. Nothing is harmed in Heaven.

I was surrounded by the most beautiful singing. Angels were singing, "Worthy is the Lamb who was slain, who is worthy to receive dominion and power forever more. Wisdom and power be given unto Thee, O Lord. Amen and Amen." You've never heard singing until you hear trillions of angels singing to the Lord. This singing meant a lot to me especially because I had earned a music degree on earth. Being in surround sound with the songs of angels was overwhelming, beyond what I can capture in mortal words to tell you.

HEAVEN'S DESIGN

Heaven is 1,500 miles in every direction. It's 250,000 square miles at its base and 780,000 stories high. There's enough room for 100 million people. The colors of the foundation stones of this city are the same as on the breastplate of Israel's high priest's garments. I saw the twelve foundational stones of the city, which were layered one on top of another as giant gem stones. The bottom foundation was of jasper, which is diamonds. Jasper stands for the glory. This is the foundational stone of the city. Each additional layer consisted of sapphires, sardis, beryl, topaz, emeralds, rubies—all different, beautiful colors, each layer another precious gem. Later, a certified scientist told me it would take seven of this world's total accumulative wealth just to garnish one of the stones I saw in the foundations. I also saw the twelve gates, one for each tribe of Israel, each made up of one solitary pearl.

An angel nodded and I was granted access to the city. The first person I saw when I entered the city was my friend John who had been decapitated in an accident in high school. His death had been a haunting memory for me. When I saw him, I was overwhelmed with joy. He was just as I remembered him only so much more complete. He ran and embraced me. It was a glorious reunion. When he wrapped his arms around me, they went all the way through me—we went into one another. This hug was so much deeper than hugs on earth.

There is a loved one assigned to show us around when we get to Heaven. John took me on a tour. We went to a library-type room with solid gold walls lined with books. There were lots of angels caring for the library. Some angels had wings, others did not—but I never saw one less than forty feet tall. Some appeared very strong and sexless—not feminine. Some had beautiful long hair. Others looked like strong, virile muscular men. They were all busy at work.

PAID IN FULL

There are volumes and volumes of books, books of souls won to the Lord, and books that contain all we have done in our lives up until we receive Jesus' forgiveness. The angels were taking these books down from the shelves, writing in them, and then replacing them.

I was able to look down on earth and see what was happening. For instance, I saw a man approach an altar and receive Jesus as His Lord and Savior. When word came back to Heaven that he received the Lord, an angel took the book with his name in it and wiped out all the transgressions in his life that he had committed up to that time. Then an angel opened the Lamb's Book of Life and wrote his name in it. The Lamb's Book is covered with lamb's wool. Then the angels went to the man's mother's mansion in Heaven and sang to her, telling her to rejoice because her son had been born again and received Jesus.

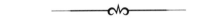

I saw the sins of others literally erased out of their books.

I saw the sins of others literally erased out of their books. I actually saw my own book and next to my name in red ink was written, "PAID IN FULL BY THE PRECIOUS BLOOD OF JESUS."

I also saw records of our spiritual growth, how we grow in our walk with the Lord as we mature, and how we respond to situations. There are records of all that.

The only way to get to Heaven is to receive Jesus, but you don't want to stop there. We should want to go on with God. I saw the names of people who were won to the Lord; also the names of the people I had led to the Lord. It is true that all we take to Heaven with us are the people whom we have impacted and influenced to bring them to Jesus.

There is one set of books in Heaven in which is recorded every person's name along with every thought, every intent, and everything we do from the moment we are born. And one day, for those who do not receive Jesus, they will be judged out of those books at the Great White Throne of Judgment. Those people will have to stand before Jesus and give an account of why they have not received Him into their lives. Jesus will say, "I could have been your advocate, your go-between, your lawyer before the Judgment Seat—but now there is evidence against you." His blood eradicates sins, but if we don't come to Him, our sins remain to testify against us.

The most important thing to the heart of God is bringing people to Jesus. I saw people in Heaven sitting on a hillside in something like bleachers watching people on earth coming to know the Lord Jesus. They were cheering for them. They were saying, "I was faithful, now you fulfill your calling and come join us." The people in Heaven can see the good things going on in earth. They are the great crowd of witnesses talked about in Hebrews 12:1, cheering on the people still on earth. They believe we'll be faithful in our walk with God and finish the race we started.

GOD INHABITS OUR PRAISE

Then I saw angels carrying bowls into the presence of God. I asked John what the angels were carrying in the bowls and he said, "The praises of God's people on the earth and Heaven above." God inhabits the praises.

Angels come and take that praise to the Father above. Those angels gather our praise and it becomes a sweet sound in the ears of the Lord.

The angels who were carrying them had six wings. With two they carry golden bowls with prayer requests and the praises of God's people and present them at the throne of God. They bow in reverence as they come into the presence of God and His power. His throne is all light, surrounded by a great aura of indescribable colors. There were peals of thunder, but there was no fear. Then the angels vanished into a fog or mist (like what dry ice produces), into the very presence of God. There were also some coming with bowls of something like water, which are the tears of the saints below. When you shed a tear, it may not be noticed on the earth, but Father God notices and keeps it on our behalf as a sweet smelling savor to Him.

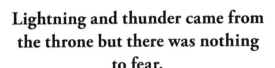

Lightning and thunder came from the throne but there was nothing to fear.

I saw seven golden lamps with fire representing the Holy Spirit. It looks like fire coming out of the lamp stand in a blaze of fire. The lamp stand represents the holiness of the city and the power of the Holy Spirit.

Then I looked and saw a magnificent crystal clear body of water flowing from the throne. Around the throne were rainbows of colors so much more intense than on earth. Lightning and thunder came from the throne but there was nothing to be fearful or afraid of.

JESUS

The first time I saw Jesus I was completely overwhelmed. As I came into His presence, I fell down before Him at His feet as a dead man. He picked me up. He was about six foot two inches tall. You don't lose your ethnic or racial origin in Heaven, so He looked Jewish, with an olive complexion. His hair was like some rabbi's—with curls along the sides of His face. He wore a regal robe of righteousness—pure white with a purple sash. Written on one side of the sash was, "King of kings," and the side read, "Lord of lords." Jesus had a solid gold belt around His waist. He was wearing a crown. I could see the indentions in His brow from where the crown of thorns had been. His eyes were deep, beautiful pools of love, and they were blue. I have since learned that Jews from the tribe of Judah are known to have blue eyes. I could see where nails had been driven into His hands, not His palms as some paintings depict, but into His wrists which would have been able to support the weight of His body. I could see where one nail went through both feet as they were crossed.

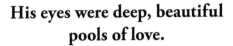

His eyes were deep, beautiful pools of love.

A radiant, beautiful light came from Him. When He looked at me, His eyes pierced me, they went all the way through me. Just pure love! I melted in His presence. He immediately started speaking to me. He gave me a message for this generation by speaking to my heart with His eyes. His words came as the same sound as the water flowing over Niagara Falls. He said, "Tell My people there's a song for them to sing, a message to proclaim, a missionary journey to take, a book to write. They all have a purpose for being here in this life." He looked at me with those piercing eyes and said, "Don't ever believe the condemnation of the devil that you are unworthy. You *are* worthy. You have been redeemed by the blood of the Lamb. Why do My people not believe in Me? Why do My people reject Me?"

His words overwhelmed me, and I was again prostrate on my face before Him. He reached down and picked me up and continued talking to me. It was like it was burned into my spirit, on the walls of my soul, like He was writing the commandments on the tablets He gave to Moses. They would now be indelibly in my spirit. "Why do they not walk in My commandments?" He asked again, not that He didn't know the answer. At that point, He commissioned me to make Him real to people on the earth. I'm a man with a message from Heaven. "Tell people they are special and unique, each one. God made every one of His children to have a divine purpose, which only they can accomplish in the earth."

I asked Him what is going on in Heaven. He told me, "I will be your focus in Heaven. You will worship and enjoy Me forever." He said, "Heaven is My creation for you. I will be the center of it all." Everything else I saw after being with Jesus was pale and dim compared to Him.

Flowers and Robes

I went to the mansion where I will spend all eternity. I opened the door and noticed that it was not ready for occupancy. I saw three buckets of paint in the living room. John dipped his hand in one of the buckets and flung the paint against the wall—flowers appeared on the wall. I walked over and picked up the whole bucket and threw the contents at the walls. Suddenly flowers appeared everywhere and the room was permeated with the sweetest floral aroma I've ever smelled. But the mansion was not ready for me to occupy.

After leaving the mansion, and walking toward the throne room, I noticed that clothing in Heaven has three different textures. A soft, velvet garment tapers to the body. It's used for everyday activities around the mansion—like we would say, around the house. The second is a robe of salvation, a garment worn on top of the first that fits to the body and is made of linen. The third garment, worn over top of that, is the "robe of righteousness" (Isa. 61:10). It is a sleeveless garment, worn in the presence of God, in the throne room. This is the "garment of praise" (Isa. 61:3 King James Version). All kinds of beautiful jewels and decorations are on this garment indicating what you did on the earth—if you were known as a writer, singer, a preacher, etc. When I saw the outer garments, I could tell what people did in their activities on the earth.

The water vitalized me, invigorated me, and gave me strength.

Then I saw coming directly from the throne room of God a magnificent river of life. My friend clothed me in a glowing, transparent robe, and we stepped into the body of water that had no bottom. The water rose like Ezekiel described. It rose up until it totally covered me. I could actually breathe in the water and interact with the water. It vitalized me, invigorated me, and gave me strength. I drank some of the water—it was so very refreshing, sweet, and rejuvenating.

I was lifted up out of the water, and I stood on the other side of the river bank. I began to see a massive group of people of all nationalities who were singing, "All hail the power of Jesus' name; let angels prostrate fall…." I asked John, "What's going on? Why are they singing the same songs we sing on earth?" John told me that all songs of the spirit originate in Heaven. So the first song I ever heard there, "Hallelujah" which is a universal song, originated in Heaven! Back on earth when I heard people singing, "Altogether lovely, altogether wonderful is He," it was sung in Heaven before I heard it on earth. Every musician and singer can receive a song from Heaven. I saw musical notes floating through the air and then go into a person who would burst into song, singing in the spirit. I also saw the notes go over the mountains that surrounded the city.

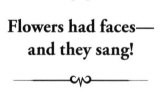

Flowers had faces— and they sang!

The angels kept rhythm to the singing, and the trees clapped and kept rhythm to the angels' singing. Everything worships God in Heaven. Everyone is exuberant and worships the Lord in some fashion. Flowers had faces and they sang. It was astounding! If people have any kind of musical background, they should allow God to use it for worship.

The streets are named Hallelujah Boulevard, Praise the Lord Avenue, and the like. We walked on transparent streets, and I could see all the way through them. A NASA scientist later told me there is an impurity in gold, and when it's removed, the gold is no longer yellow, it's crystal clear. As we walked, I saw a playground with children and teenagers—those who died prematurely. I also saw massive lumps of clay, and I saw angels working with smaller clumps of clay. They were forming and fashioning it as if they were sculpting. I asked John what they were making. He said they were for miscarried or aborted babies and were being formed and fashioned to what God wants them to be. In another area were children petting lions like they were harmless kittens. One little girl ran and jumped into the arms of Jesus. Most of the time I was in Heaven, I saw Jesus spending time with children and teens.

THE PARTS ROOM

One of my favorite parts of the whole experience is the Parts Room. About five hundred yards from the throne room, there is a storage room. On the door a sign reads, "Unclaimed Blessings." I opened the door, and I was blown away. There were legs hanging from the walls. Every part of one's anatomy was stored in that room. God has a spare parts room. God has miracles just waiting to give to people. Then I saw people on the earth pray, and I saw the prayers come up to Heaven.

The angels received the prayers and retrieved that specific miracle, that new part for the ears, spinal column, or a new kidney from the Parts Room, and they took the part to the person who needed it. Many times they had to fight principalities and powers. I saw how the enemy hinders those prayers and discourages the people praying. The angels were released to get the miracles and to deliver the miracles, but the people had given up, thinking they would never receive their miracles.

I remembered that Daniel had to wait twenty-one days for the angel to come to him with the manifestation of his prayer. The angel left Heaven the minute Daniel prayed, but the angel was hindered so it took awhile. People negate their miracles by saying, "It's not for me," or "It's not the day of miracles." There is no "day of miracles." There is a *God of miracles!*

Our God is without limitations. Everything we get from God comes on the wings of faith. We receive healing by faith. Our faith makes us whole. The earth's atmosphere is where Satan rules, and where evil spirits target people and try to deceive them. When people get on their knees or begin to pray and direct their prayers to Heaven in Jesus' name, the prayers go into Heaven like sharp, barbed arrows. A whole army of angelic forces come and cause the demonic forces to retreat.

When believers declare, "It is written," then you can say, "It is finished. The Word of God says it is written. I believe it, I accept it, and it's finished." When people pray like that, the angels go into battle for them. That's why it is so important to stand on God's Word as a basis for prayer. An army of angels is prepared to battle demons based on prayer. When two or more people agree, it increases angel activity. There is an increase of angel activity in this day in which we live. We should count on their help.

An army of angels is prepared to battle demons based on prayer.

When I was with Jesus and He spoke to me about what He wanted me to share back on the earth, He also told me that there would be a time of restoration on the earth that would be more than the Azusa Street Revival. Also, it is time to get ready for His return, to get all the sin out of our lives. This message was really why I was sent back. I was receiving information that Jesus was giving to me and instructing me about my assignment. Everyone has an assignment and a purpose. Even a salesperson's purpose is to talk about Jesus. Everyone has a destiny to be fulfilled.

GOING BACK

I also had to go back to earth because my little sister, who was in the accident with me, was praying for my life in Jesus' name. My friend John said, "You have to go back, she's using the Name." His name is more powerful than death, than cancer. There's power in the name of Jesus. Although they were working on her to stop the bleeding, she was praying for me. I had been pronounced dead twenty minutes earlier, yet she was still praying.

The next moment, I was catapulted back into my body. Because I was dead for twenty minutes and without oxygen for that long, I was brain dead—yet I knew I still had all my faculties. I heard a doctor say, "He will never speak or sing again." I needed a miracle.

A few days later, I heard a song I had never heard before: "He touched me and made me whole." In my mind I prayed, "Lord, what that song says, You can do." Suddenly Jesus appeared in my hospital room just as He looked in Heaven. I was filled with awe at His beautiful presence. He put His gentle hand on my throat. I felt warmth spread through my body. He smiled at me and left the room. A nurse came in and said, "How are you this morning?" I threw my hands up and said, "Praise God, I've been healed!" She dropped the tray and ran and got the doctors. They said, "It's impossible. You can't speak."

But when Jesus comes, everything changes! I got a second opinion. Dr. Jesus said I could. I have a Word that supersedes what the doctors have to say, *"by His wounds I am healed!"* (see 1 Pet. 2:24).

Commentary

Gary's encounters with Jesus make us long to see Him, long to be near Him, to hear Him speak to us personally. Jesus commissioned Gary to return to earth with a personal message for you! God created you to do what only you can do. Each person has been created for a specific purpose and that includes you. As Jesus spoke to Gary, an additional message comes to us from Him: Do not believe the lies of the devil who brings condemnation and tells us we're not worthy. When we believe the lie that we're not worthy, we are disbelieving God who says He has made us worthy of all He wants to give to us, by the blood of Jesus. God says we're worthy and equipped, and He says we each have a part to play. We can share the love and the truth of the Lord with others in some way that is unique to us.

Gary confirms that every thought or intention we have ever had from the time we were born is recorded in Heaven by angels. We are comforted by the assurance that all of our sins, from the least unkind thought we have ever had to the worst of our transgressions, is wiped away and God has no more remembrance of them. Our sins are as if they never existed. For all eternity, next to our names in the Lamb's Book of Life is written in red, PAID IN FULL BY THE PRECIOUS BLOOD OF JESUS.

Never again can there be a charge against God's chosen ones. If Jesus has forgiven us, how can we not forgive anyone who has hurt us or someone we love if we call ourselves followers of Jesus? No wonder there is such joy in Heaven. Imagine, every aspect of fallen humanity is no longer ascribed to you or part of your life in any way. Because of the atoning blood of Jesus, this is our legal status with God—a new life in Spirit and in truth.

> *...anyone united with the Messiah gets a fresh start,* [and] *is created new. The old life is gone; a new life burgeons! Look at it! All this comes from the God who settled the relationship between us and him, and then called us to settle our relationships with each other...* (2 Corinthians 5:17,19 The Message).

About Dr. Gary Wood

Sensing the call of God on his life from a young age, Gary was preparing to preach and sing the gospel when a fatal automobile accident took his life, sending him to Heaven to the feet of Jesus. After allowing Gary profound experiences in Heaven, Jesus commissioned Gary to make Him real to people wherever he went. Gary has been traveling the world as an evangelist with this message ever since. He is the author of *A Place Called Heaven.*

CHAPTER 7

BEFORE THE THRONE OF GOD

Robert Misst

In September 2010, Bob attended a week-end prayer retreat in Christchurch, New Zealand. As they began to worship, the Lord interrupted their worship, and He let them know that they were worshiping in the "old way"—and you can't enter into the new things of God with "old baggage." Bob was about to find out what that meant.

We had just started singing our first song of worship when I noticed that the sounds in the room were suddenly shut off. I could not hear the music or the people singing. I was being escorted from a place of darkness, a tunnel, toward a bright light. I felt the presence of an angel with me, escorting me toward that light. I felt the angel's hand on my right shoulder, which means the angel was on my left side. In the dark tunnel, I could not see the face of the angel.

We moved toward the light; and as we came closer, I began to see what was happening there in the light. I first noticed huge angels flying around a massive area, the ends of which I could not really discern. The size and countenance of the angels brought the fear of God in me; there was something so holy about them. I suddenly realized that I was so sinful, my garments were dirty, and I could not be in this place. I tried to move backward, hoping that these huge flying angels did not notice me in this holy place. The angel who escorted me to this place held my shoulder, preventing me from taking a backward step. I heard his assurance.

Then I heard God's heavenly beings speaking to me, I heard it not with my ears, but in the center of my head, like a spiritual download straight to my brain! I now knew that I had been brought to the courts of the heavenly temple of God.

While I was perceiving many things happening all together, I can only write about them one experience at a time. This whole place was exuberant with the holiness of God, as they sang "Holy, Holy, Holy is the Lord, who was and is and is to come." The escorting angel said to me, "These are the cherubim. They are the guardians of the Mercy Seat of God." The cherubim were very large angelic beings that flew around this vast heavenly temple where the worship was going on. (I am calling it a temple—no one ever told me that in Heaven.) I was afraid of the cherubim because of their sheer size and the awesome features of their faces. It was as if I these beings were so filled with the mind of God and the intent to do the will of God, that just staring into those eyes could disintegrate my entire sinful being into nothingness.

They had more than two pairs of wings—it was hard for me to count how many pairs of wings as they flew around the throne of God. Also, I was afraid to make eye contact with them. I wanted to leave the place and did not want to be seen by them. Every time they called out, "Holy, Holy, Holy...," it was like the entire temple reverberated with their voices and the entire place was filled with the awesome holiness of God. This is hard to explain as only our spirits can perceive a place that is filled with the awesome holiness of God that made me want to lay prostrate and bow as low as possible. I felt as if my garments were dirty, as if I should not be in this place of such holiness of God.

Two Groups

I then noticed a small group of people in very stately attire some distance below the huge flying angels. I did not count the number of them, but later the escorting angel explained this to me. Something about the people made me want to cry. Their whole body language spoke to me of their holiness, love, humility, caution in approaching God, passion for the One whom they serve, and the dedication in their service to Him. They wore crowns on their heads. The escorting angel said, "These are the twenty-four elders." They looked like humans, and definitely not angelic beings. I did not recognize any of them as characters in the Bible like Moses, or Abraham, or any of the apostles. But who can say what Moses, or Abraham or even the apostles looked like? The elders in Heaven represent Jewish people who have accepted *Yeshua HaMashiach* (Jesus the Messiah, the Anointed One), and the born-again Gentiles. This is a picture of the end-time church, the "One New Man" in Messiah, Jew and Gentile worshiping together. (See Ephesians 2:14-15.)

Beyond this circle of people in stately attire with crowns on their heads was a vast group of people, too numerous to even estimate. My attention was drawn to the way they were grouped, which displayed something so unique, so special about them. It was like a special identity that had richness about them, and it was also like a gift they brought with them to offer to God. But what awed me is that their body language expressed a deep love, holiness, and passion for the One they had come into this place to worship. The escorting angel informed me that these people were from every tribe and nation and tongue. I was awed by the myriads of angels just above them, but lower than the cherubim. Their numbers looked like billion times billion, and they created a holy anticipation of the One who was to come into their midst.

Seeing all this kept reminding me of my dirty garments as compared to the stately robes with which this holy assembly was adorned. I wanted to back off from this place, with the hope that no one had noticed me. The escorting angel pressed my shoulder to tell me he was with me, and not to be afraid. He was very assuring that I needed to be there, and that his assignment was to escort me and show me around.

In the center of this circle of people in beautiful robes, is a bright light; and I could see a throne almost in outline, as I tried to peer into this beautiful light. As I mentioned previously, there was such a bright light emitting from the throne that it was hard for me to see it in all its splendor—maybe the heavenly beings can see it that way, in all its heavenly splendor. I could barely discern the outline of the throne. Above it was a circular rainbow, like a halo around the throne. Seven different musical instruments were "painting" the seven colors of the rainbow with their sound! Flashes of lightning and peals of thunder filled the atmosphere with a tangible holiness as God and His Beloved Son, our Lord Jesus, entered the throne room.

The throne around which these mighty cherubim flew, I was told by the escorting angel, was God's mercy seat. Moses was instructed by God to build the Ark of the Covenant that had the mercy seat of God covered with the wings of the cherubim. The mercy seat was not easily discernable by my eyes for it also emitted a glowing light. I could barely perceive the outline of God's mercy seat.

Since I began to understand that the escorting angel had brought me into the throne room of God, the place of worship in Heaven where the heavenly bride worships God, I was not surprised to see God's throne, but I was surprised that I could not see it clearly due to the light emitting from it. The entire environment had an awesome holiness about it—a place where no sin can reside in the heart and mind of all those heavenly beings around God's throne worshiping Him. This is the quality of holiness where no sin is found. I can understand why Satan was cast out of God's presence.

I was caught up by the strange shapes of exquisite beauty in the place, the likes of which I had never seen on the earth, not even in pictures or in artistic impressions. The escorting angel showed me objects that emitted sound and color and told me that the heavenly temple is filled with objects that have the ability to resonate with heavenly music based on the music harmonies that come from our voices. I hummed a short tune to try this out, and I was amazed at the sound that matched the tune of my humming and played a number of beautiful intersecting improvisations.

COLORFUL SOUNDS

Suddenly I was able to hear the worship in the holy heavenly temple. If I had been in my mortal body, I could have died just from the beauty of the sound. Then I was ushered into the throne room, and suddenly my vulnerable being was subjected to seven-layered multiple chorus choirs that have over a billion voices singing. Add to that the sound and colors being emitted by these awesome musical instruments and in the midst of this awesome worship in sound and song, I could see and hear the lightning and thunder that emitted from the throne itself. I was consumed by the beauty of the worship and the joy that flooded my soul—but also the desire to run away as I was not holy enough to stand in this place. I wanted to hide, or I thought I would die!

I could have died just from the beauty of the sound.

The cherubim sang their song: "Holy, Holy, Holy is the Lord." I began to notice that each of the groups in the heavenly temple had their own song or chorus. I was hearing multiple choruses all at the same time, yet in perfect harmony. Added to these multiple choruses were the perfect music harmonies played by these beautiful instruments, which I had never seen on the earth. I was awed beyond words, basking in the most glorious worship in Heaven. There were other earthly sounds that hit my ear, depending on the choruses, the sound of distant thunder, peals of lightning, and the sound of wind and water, all at the same time, all blending together harmoniously.

I then saw a figure emerging from the light emitted from the throne, a Person dressed in the most brilliant attire. I was told by the escorting angel that He is Jesus, the Lamb of God. I was filled with the fear of God and almost did not want to look, for in His entire being was the exuberance of love and mercy that shone forth like no star in Heaven could. The twenty-four elders who surrounded the throne tore away the crowns from their heads and cast them on the ground before Him. They prostrated themselves before the Lamb of God. He moved with such gentleness, love, and mercy toward the elders and lifted them to their feet. In the gaze of each other, the Lord toward the twenty-four elders and they toward Him, were the most profound, deep expressions of love, honor, respect, and holiness. The Lamb of God gently picked up the crowns to place them on the head of each elder. I was permitted to hear an elder say, "No Lord, only You are worthy to wear the crown." I could see in their expressions that the elders' love for the Lamb was far more important than the crowns and all that crowns signify.

After Jesus, the Lamb of God, put the crowns on all the elders' heads, He asked one of the elders, pointing to the vast group of people from the tribes and tongues and nations, who those people are, and the elder said, *"These are the ones who come out of the great tribulation, and they have washed their robes and made them white in the blood of the Lamb"* (Rev. 7:14). The Lamb of God moved to one of them and placed a crown on the person's head. The person refused to accept the crown saying, "Only You are worthy, Lord, to wear the crown." This person then said to the Lamb of God, "There are many on the earth who still need to be saved; we are not worthy to wear the crown." The Lamb of God then assured the person, "As you worship Me, I will set the people on the earth free." The Lamb of God embraced the person, and His embrace touched me so deeply in the way He expresses His holy love and honor and respect for each person.

As the Lamb of God, one would expect Him to be seated on His throne and receiving all the glory and pomp and splendor as earthly kings and queens normally strut around waiting to be served. But here I saw God in all His glory go to the heavenly beings, pick them up from their prostrate position, pick up their crowns, and place each one on their heads—something one does not expect a person of high stature to do. Yet in the Lord Jesus, we witness a King who is majesty, love, and mercy, and still One who serves because it is His character and nature to do so, even in His omniscience!

WORSHIP HAS A PURPOSE

The escorting angel began to speak to me about the worship in Heaven. He taught me that worship in Heaven has a purpose. Each chorus sung by each group has a purpose. The purpose of all the worship in the heavenly temple moves the end-time purposes of God on earth. I was shown in the heavenly temple that each of the choruses sung by each of seven groups has a message for the church in the following manner:

The song of the cherubim: The chorus of the four living creatures, the cherubim, sing, "Holy, Holy, Holy, is the Lord God, the Almighty, who was and who is and who is to come."

The song the elders around the throne of God sing is, "Worthy are You, our Lord and our God, to receive glory and honor and power; for You created all things, and because of Your will they existed, and were created."

The song of the bride is the calling or declarations by the nations about the beauty of the Lord, desiring to be with Him. "The Spirit and Bride say (sing), 'Come.'"

The song of the angels: The new song of Heaven is "Worthy is the Lamb who was slain to receive power and riches and wisdom and might and honor and glory and blessing."

The song of the tribes and nations: The earth synergizes with Heaven in the song of the tribes and nations, singing, "To Him who sits on the throne and to the Lamb be praise and honor and glory and power, forever and ever!"

The song of creation: The victorious song of the over-comers, the "one sound" of Heaven and earth is The Song of Moses: "Salvation belongs to our God!"

The great thanksgiving song: The great three-fold *"Hallelujah!"*

I then saw the Lamb of God taking the scroll and breaking the first seal. I had no idea what was happening. The worship was still in a deep place, and the twenty-four elders were now holding golden bowls of incense as they were praying. I could not distinctly hear their prayers. The escorting angel explained that they were saying to Him, "Lord, the time has come for the marriage of the Lamb. Will You not do this for the sake of Your bride on earth and in Heaven? Will You not break the seals and start the processes that will lead to the marriage feast?"

The Lamb seemed to be waiting for something that would signal the breaking of the seals. He is waiting to hear the voice of His bride on the earth asking Him to come soon to the earth, to prepare Heaven for their dwelling place and for the marriage to take place! The Lamb took the scroll and broke open the first seal. There was a great sigh, and sounds like holy cheers arose from the tribes and tongues and nations.

Almost immediately one of the mighty cherubim called out in a thunderous loud voice that shook me to the very atoms of my body. He said, "Come forth," and a white horse with an angelic rider presented itself before the entire assembly. The Lamb spoke to the rider and sent the angel forth with a great command on the holy assignment. I was allowed to see four seals broken by the Lamb amid profound worship, intercession, and the sounds of warfare taking place in the heavenly temple.

Four angelic beings rode on horses, the first being white, the second red, the third black, and the fourth on a pale green horse. I was not permitted to hear their assignments but was assured by the angel that I would be told in time. Before I could wonder when that time could be, suddenly the lights in the heavenly temple seemed to go out, and I found myself back in the prayer room with the others staring at me. When I opened my eyes, they wanted to know what vision I had just seen. The vision had seemed like all eternity had passed before my eyes.

The Lord has since released revelation as to the understanding of the vision experience. I now understand it better and participate in it by joining Heaven in their worship, warfare, and intercession. This is what the Lord Jesus, the Lamb of God, is seeking from His bride on the earth—participation in what He is doing for the restoration and renewal processes of the earth.

Commentary

Being in the Lord's presence in all His holiness caused Bob to be aware of his own sense of unworthiness. This was mirrored by the elders in Heaven who cast the crowns given them by the Lamb of God at His feet, saying that only He is truly worthy of all praise. Whether in Heaven or on the earth, when in His presence, we are awed and greatly humbled by His holiness. Bob was taught that the key word in understanding worship is humility. As the Lamb, who is also Almighty God, came to each one of the elders with such love, honor, and respect, we are again humbled by this revelation of the majesty of humility that is profoundly resident in God Himself.

God took Bob to Heaven in the vision to teach him to pray in a way that would accomplish the highest will of God. Worship should be inseparable from our prayers. Bob was taught that worship belongs to God. Therefore, our concern should be to touch the heart of God and to pray in tandem with Heaven.

Praying primarily through situations and for our concerns would appear to be earthbound and situational when God is waiting to hear the voices of His beloved bride telling Him that we long for Him, asking Him to come to us, and to do what needs to be done to make all things ready for His return. While we are longing for Him, He is longing for us, to have His bride on earth join with the worshipers in Heaven for His highest will to be fully accomplished.

If we wish to see God's highest will done in our lives and in the earth, the way to pray would be to align our desires with God's desires so that our focus is on the Lord and His ultimate issues, to pray according to Scriptures that define His will for the earth. As we seek Him and His righteousness, He will take care of the rest that concerns us. When our treasure, all that we truly value, is in Heaven, the cares of this world will greatly diminish, our expectations and faith will keep us close to the Lord's intimate presence, and we will be praying God's highest will.

> ..."*Worthy is the Lamb that was slain to receive power and riches and wisdom and might and honor and glory and blessing.*" *And every created thing which is in heaven and on the earth and under the earth and on the sea, and all things in them, I heard saying, "To Him who sits on the throne, and to the Lamb, be blessing and honor and glory and dominion forever and ever*" (Revelation 5:11-13).

> *Come, Lord Jesus. The grace of the Lord Jesus Christ be with* [you] *all. Amen* (Revelation 22:20b-21).

About Robert Misst

Bob was a well thought out atheist until he met the Lord Jesus in 1974. After struggling to surrender his life completely to Jesus, he subsequently served in several renewal programs and helped establish a church in Mumbai, India. In 1987, Jesus called him into prophetic intercession for the nations. He and his team traveled throughout India holding prophetic intercession vigils to which up to 1,500 would come to prayerfully intercede for their city, their country, and for the nations. Bob has linked with other intercessory prayer teams while traveling around the world.

In 2002, the Lord called Bob to move to New Zealand to pray for that nation. He also works with the leadership of the National Days of Prayer network and conducts seminars on "Worship, Warfare, and Intercession" to prepare for the return of the Lord Jesus. He is author of *Worship, Warfare & Intercession: Before the Throne of God*.

CHAPTER 8

A PICTURE OF LIFE IN HEAVEN

Richard Sigmund

Richard's great-grandfather was a Jewish circuit preacher during the Civil War and Richard's grandfather would talk to him about the Lord Jesus being Israel's Messiah. God spoke to Richard when he was four years old. A voice called his name. Then a cloud came down and out of the cloud came a stairway. Jesus walked down the stairway and took Richard by the hand. He said, "You will preach the gospel, heal the sick, and the dead shall be raised. Remember, I've called you to preach. Your life will not be like other little boys." Then He went up the stairs, and the cloud went up with Him. Richard began preaching shortly after that day and served Him faithfully from then on. Years later,

*suddenly, an accident for which there seemed
no cause took his life.*

I died in an auto accident, though there was no sign of any oncoming car or evidence revealing any cause for the accident. No one ever discovered a reason for the accident. Evidently, I died instantly. When they pulled me out of the car, nearly every bone in my body was broken, including my back, neck, and both arms. Two ribs went through my heart. The medics said I had been dead for about eight hours when they found me.

In the first remembrance I have of leaving my body, I was going through a thick veil that tasted like honey. As I was going through it, it was going through me. I was propelled by some unseen force. I felt so wonderful and at great peace. At first I didn't know what happened, but as I neared the edge of the veil, I heard voices on the other side. Once through the veil I turned and saw a group of people. They were singing and praising God. I heard voices say, "He is coming. I see him. He's coming. Here he comes." Suddenly a man came through the veil. He had a look of profound confusion for a moment. He didn't know where he was. But just as suddenly, he looked at the group and recognized them. They began to hug him and to praise and worship God. What a joyous reunion.

Then I heard someone say, "There she is." A person in the group was carrying a baby. The baby had the full power of speech. The baby cried with a baby voice,

"Mommy! Mommy! There is my mommy." (I learned that Jesus said the baby could remain a baby and that his mommy could raise him in Heaven.) At that moment, an old, wrinkled woman, stooped shouldered and very frail came through the veil. Instantly upon entering the atmosphere of Heaven, she snapped completely straight. Suddenly she was once again a beautiful young woman, dressed in a radiant, pure white robe of glory. Everyone cheered with shouts of joy as the baby flew into her arms. They had been parted at childbirth. The woman had survived a concentration camp, but her baby had not. Yet God, in His infinite mercy, saw to it that nothing was lost. How great is the love of God! *I must be in Heaven,* I thought. *What a wonderful place to be.*

Walk on this Path

Next, I was standing on a golden pathway. I heard a voice say, "You must walk on this path." The voice sounded familiar to me. I knew it was the voice of Jesus though I didn't see Him then. Beside me stood two angels who would always accompany me. On either side of the path was the richest turf-green grass I'd ever seen. It was moving with life and energy. There were flowers of every imaginable size and color along the path on which I was now walking. I saw roses that were about four feet across. As I walked, the flowers faced me and they were all humming. The air was filled with their aroma. I asked the angels if I could pick one to smell it and I was told

I could. When I put the flower down, it replanted itself. There is no death in Heaven, not of anything.

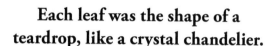

Each leaf was the shape of a teardrop, like a crystal chandelier.

As I walked along the path with the angels, I noticed the sky. It was pinkish in color, with clouds of glory. When I looked more closely, I saw that the clouds were made up of thousands and thousands of people in groups singing. They were strolling in the sky. The beautifully manicured grounds were filled with huge, striking trees that must have been at least two thousand feet tall and of many different varieties. One tree caught my attention. It seemed to be miles across. I was told it was a diadem tree. Each leaf was the shape of a teardrop, like a crystal chandelier. There was a continual sound of chimes coming from the leaves as they brushed against one another. The tree glowed with light and sound. It became aflame with glory. The flame started in the root and went all the way through the branches and out into the chandelier-like leaves. The tree exploded in a cloud of glory—a beautiful light and an unbelievably beautiful sound. The diadem tree was glorious.

Under it were what looked like tens of thousands of people worshiping, but they were not worshiping the tree, only God. The closer I got to the throne room, the more trees I saw and each was as glorious as the diadem tree. I went to one tree that had fruit. When I picked a fruit from it another one grew immediately in its place. When I put the fruit to my lips, it melted into the most delicious thing I have ever tasted. It was like honey and peach juice and pear juice all at the same time, sweet, but not sugary. The trees gave off a beautiful aroma. I was told to take a leaf and smell it, and I did. Then a voice told me that it would give me strength to carry on. The moment I smelled the beautiful fragrance, I was strengthened.

HEAVEN'S ARCHIVES

I was then taken to the archives of Heaven. It was a large building, miles tall, deep and wide. Inside this building were layers of bookshelves; I do not know how tall. Angels were stationed all around these books. A large angel held a book at about shoulder level to me. It was about fifteen feet square and two feet thick. It must have weighed a ton. He opened one third of the way through the book and showed it to me. It had a picture of me looking at the angel holding the book. I saw in the book what was going on at that moment. I saw another angel, a huge angel, who had open a golden book with a quill-like writing instrument that was about six feet long. He was looking and writing, looking and writing. The pen could write forever!

I asked the angel with me what the other angel was doing. He told me the history of each life, everything past, present, and future that is under the blood of Jesus and forgiven is in those books. Angels record all that is done and said on earth, and even our thoughts are recorded. Nothing remains of sin for those whose names have been cleansed by the precious blood of Jesus, the Lamb of God. I understood that's why it's important to keep a pure mind. The eye is the window of our soul. Thoughts enter our souls through what we look at. That's why it's important to guard what we see, to guard our spirits.

The good things you make happen on earth will happen to you in Heaven.

I was also taken to see the Rewards Department in Heaven. It is another huge building where records are kept of the rewards that we do not receive on earth for some reason or another. An example would be the reward for giving to others because of love and compassion we have in our hearts, or to give to a greater need than our own. What we give on earth we will receive back in Heaven. God desires to bless us even more than we desire to be blessed by Him. God has plans to bless you even more than you've ever been a blessing to others.

The good things you make happen on earth will happen to you in Heaven.

One of the books in the Rewards Department contains desires, wants, and wishes of believers while on earth. They may not have been fulfilled on earth, but they will be in Heaven. Plans are being laid in Heaven according to what is written in the book. There are heavenly events in store for you.

THE HOLY SPIRIT

I saw multitudes of angels in another place who are given to us for wisdom. They go to the library of God's knowledge to get wisdom and bring it to us, or they go with a special instruction to bring it and cause it to happen on earth. I also saw that the Holy Spirit was in charge of it all—He leads, He guides, He directs, and He gives instruction to the angels who do not act on their own but only under the order of the Lord Jesus and the power of the Holy Spirit. Only the name of Jesus can loose the angels for us. When we mention the name of Jesus in our prayers, the Holy Spirit immediately begins to direct the action and the angels of God come into play for us. I saw that each person who is born again has not one angel, but two. It is important that we, as the children of God, allow God to go into action for us.

When you get to Heaven there's no such thing as a wounded soul. You are in absolute tranquility and peace.

There are no bad thoughts, the only thing you have is a desire to worship God and be a blessing to someone else. On earth we have wounding and wounded souls; in Heaven, we have only blessings. The people in Heaven don't have the souls we do on earth.

As we continued to walk, the angels beside me, I saw a three-level mansion of maybe thirty rooms. There I saw my grandfather and my grandmother sitting on the porch together talking to other people walking by. I wasn't allowed to talk to my grandfather, but he saw me and he waved and smiled a great big smile. That meant everything to me.

THE THRONE ROOM

Again I heard a voice say, "You have an appointment with God." I knew that voice was the voice of Jesus. His sheep know His voice. I was escorted to the enormous throne room. It was wider and higher than I could even imagine—hundreds of miles, with massive arches and pillars. Everything in Heaven comes out of the throne. Everything in existence revolves around the throne.

I could feel a difference as I approached the throne. As I got nearer to it, the air became electrically charged with the power and presence of God. It sounded like a hundred million dynamos (Greek: *dynamis*, from which we get the word dynamite) of power was coming out from the throne. It took me awhile to get used to the atmosphere. God is so intently God that I couldn't go easily before Him—I thought I would vaporize. I had to condition myself to the atmosphere there. The closer I got to the throne, the greater the wonders.

The throne room of God is the most beautiful place in Heaven.

The closer I got to the throne, the more everything became transparent. Everything is absolutely transparent, with purity closest to God. I saw Jesus walk up to the throne and disappear into the enfolding fire that surrounds the Being on the throne. I saw Him at the throne, and I saw Him in the throne. I didn't see Father God, but I did see His foot, His toe. He is a very big God! Jesus walked in and out of the glory. It was awesome. The throne room of God is the most beautiful spot in Heaven.

Later, after leaving the throne room, I did see Jesus again from afar talking to different groups of people here and there. He seems to be everywhere. Children run to Him continually, and He loves them all. Then I saw Jesus close to me. When I saw Him, I stopped and the angels stood at attention and backed away from me a couple of feet. Then they bowed low, backed up some more and stood at attention with looks of adoration on their faces. Then Jesus walked toward me. He stopped a few feet from me, and I fell on my face like a dead man. I remember looking at the nail holes through His feet. They shone with a light from the inside of beautiful, beautiful Jesus. He suffered this for me! I had no words.

He touched me, and I was able to stand. I did not feel worthy to stand or look at His face. He reached out His fingers, lifted my chin and said, "Son, look at Me. I love you. Even though you have been disobedient and haven't done what I have told you to do, I still love you, and I desire for you to tell My people the glorious things that My Father has made for them."

He took my hand and began to walk with me like a father would a little child. We walked a little farther and He said, "Tell My people I am coming soon. And I love them." Then He gave me a big hug and kissed me on the cheek and said, "I love you, too." He held out His hands in front of me, and I saw where the nails pierced Him. The wounds were open, and yet shining through them was a beautiful light. I saw my name written in His hand, looking almost as if a knife had carved it in there. "See," He said, "your name is carved on My hand." I knew the Scripture that says, *"Behold, I have inscribed you on the palms of My hands..."* (Isa. 49:16). Then suddenly He was gone and the angels came back around me.

Warfaring Angels

I was then taken to a very large area that wasn't in the city. I don't know where it was and I don't know what part of Heaven it was in, but I was taken there in an instant. I was in the air, and I looked down on possibly hundreds of thousands of angels lined up in ranks and in units. They looked like soldiers getting ready to go on parade. Then I knew supernaturally that they were standing right where they had been positioned by God when He first created them for His purposes. They were God's warfaring angels—they leave Heaven to fight battles for us on earth. Then they go back to Heaven until they are needed again. Some of them had swords that looked fifteen feet long and were on fire. The swords were made of flaming materials.

These angels were not tall and slender, as I'd seen elsewhere in Heaven. Nor were they friendly or kindly looking, like other angels. These were fearsome angels dressed in battle garb. They didn't have helmets, but they had huge shields, flaming swords and spears that were about thirty feet long. They must have stood twenty feet tall and weighed the better part of a ton, according to earthly measure. They were huge, muscular angels. They looked like Mr. America but considerably larger. They had supernatural weapons that I do not know how to explain. I knew that some of them could speak words and cause whole nations to crumble and fall into the sea.

———————— ⟡ ————————

"Behold the warfaring angels of God. They are mighty to pull down the strongholds of the evil one."

———————— ⟡ ————————

They were armed, some with words, some with swords, some with spears for special purposes, and all with the power of God. They knew their jobs—their highly specialized jobs—and how to do them. They didn't need to be told *how* to do their job; God just needed to tell them *where* to do them. As I looked at them, one of the angels standing with me said, "Behold the warfaring angels of God. They are mighty to pull down the strongholds of the evil one."

I noticed that their hands were clothed with power and I asked, "Why are their hands aflame?" I was told that they are ready at any moment to come and do battle against the power of the devil that assails us. The power of God is in their hands to do all that He wants them to do. They are released to fight for us the minute we mention the name of Jesus. I saw thousands of them come out of ranks almost at the speed of light and disappear. I knew they were going to earth to help someone. Oh, the power of God that is available for us! If we only knew how much the angels have to do with our victory on earth and how God wants us to have victory—all the time!

Then one of my angels said, "Come. You have another appointment with Jesus," as he bowed his head in complete humility. "Come, now. The Master awaits." I was taken to the Rose Garden. The Rose Garden is God's personal place in Heaven—His favorite place. The roses were quite large and burst into a thousand different colors beyond description. Most of the colors would be impossible to capture on earth. There in the center was a sitting place with garden furniture made of solid gold. Jesus was sitting there waiting for me. Again, I fell at His feet, and the only sound I could utter was a very weak, "My Lord and Savior." I was weeping with great joy.

Everything in Heaven seems to stand still when the Lord Jesus speaks. A hand as strong as steel lifted me up and I was looking into the Master's face. He gave me a loving, all-knowing look of absolute acceptance. I was trembling with ecstasy.

He said, "Sit down." He stood and talked to me. "I must tell you," He said, "that I'm coming back for My people."

I said, "They know that."

Jesus said, "No they don't. They're asleep. They're at ease. I'm coming as a thief in the night. I'm sending you back to herald My return. I am coming back for people who make themselves ready, for those who lay aside every sin and get their eyes totally upon Me. I am the Way, the Truth, and the Life." When He said that, it was as if all Heaven joined in and said, "Amen."

Then Jesus drew back a few steps and began to speak. "For centuries, men have tried to interpret My Word. Some were correct, in as much light as they had. Some were wrong, and some of them were sent by the evil one to lead My Father's creation astray. From the day that My grace was extended to redeem creation, the evil one has tried to steal it from My hands. But until the day that I will soon return, that which My Father has committed to Me will not be taken from Me. I have worked to make salvation available to all.

"I was there when the first rays of My glory created the universe. I was there when the planets were made. I did it. I created everything to work perfectly after its own order. I fellowshipped with the first created man in these gardens—until sin became a reality. Into outer darkness My Father cast the evil one and all those who followed him. They were cast far away from this perfect abode that I have prepared for My bride of faithful believers. The days of creation are numbered. My Father alone knows the number of days. He alone. Soon, I will take the heavenly armies that you have witnessed, along with these elders who are here, and go get My people. It will be the happiest time of all eternity," He said.

"You will go back," He told me.

Immediately I began to weep at the thought. It hurt so. He reached out and touched my shoulder and great peace came again. "Go tell My people what you have seen here. And tell them to get their lives clean and full of My Spirit. Only with My help can they endure to the end." Jesus said again, "You're going back."

I sighed and He rebuked me. "The will of My Father is never grievous. Stand to your feet. You must go back. You will come back to Heaven," He said. Then Jesus hugged me.

Suddenly my body was full of pain and there was a sheet over my face. I could feel my bones knitting together. I heard a voice say, "He's been dead all these hours. It's about time to embalm him."

I sat up and said, "I ain't dead yet." Someone hollered, "He's alive! That dead man is alive!" A doctor came in and said, "I pronounced him dead, and he's dead." But I was sitting up, breathing, and talking. Other doctors and nurses came in the room and I began to tell them what had happened. People were weeping at what I was saying about my trip to Heaven.

The doctors agreed, "This must be a miracle of God."

Commentary

Richard Sigmund is now with the Lord permanently. He will never have to leave again. But the message he was sent back to tell people remains as an inspiration and a hope. When I interviewed Richard before he went to be with the Lord, anytime he would say the name of Jesus he would say it with the most tenderhearted reverence. Richard's story presents to us what appears to be a rare almost word-for-word account of a conversation with Jesus Himself. We see how much He wants to protect us and to bless us. He is so intimately involved with us, that our every thought and intention is captured and written down. This story confirms again that there is no record of sins once we come to the Lord. Once the blood of Jesus has washed away our sins, meticulous records are kept of our lives because God is looking for ways to reward us for acts of love and kindness that we do to bless others or the intentions of our hearts to bless and honor God.

Knowing of this acceptance we have in God stirs within us a desire to live to please God far beyond any need to please men in order to gain acceptance or applause. In fact, the more you know the Lord Jesus, the more uncomfortable you become with praise that goes to anyone other than the Lord Himself. God wants to bless us and is making plans in Heaven to meet our deepest desires and longings. While we're here on earth, that God has mighty angels to help us, to protect us, to rescue us, is unquestionable from what we've seen from these heavenly accounts. The insights God has provided for us through these stories bring to us a confidence in God and the name of Jesus that leaves no room for fear or insecurity in God. We are not here on earth alone. We have the Holy Spirit; we also have the angels who are diligently working to care for each of us as the Lord directs them. Nothing we do on earth or that concerns us is outside of God's involvement, His power, or His love.

> *Seeing that His divine power has granted to us everything pertaining to life and godliness, through the true knowledge of Him who called us by His own glory and excellence* (2 Peter 1:3).

About Richard Sigmund

Richard's grandfather was praying while Richard was being born in Des Moines, Iowa, and the Lord told him, "Through him I will answer prayer." The prayer that was being answered was that of his great-grandfather, a Spirit-filled Jewish circuit riding preacher during the Civil War. The Lord first appeared to Richard when he was four years old. He began preaching with Reverend Jack Coe Sr. at age five. At nine, he began preaching with healing evangelist A.A. Allen, which he did for ten years and also presented his testimony during meetings of William Branham. In his early twenties, Richard held fruitful tent meetings among the Navajo First Nation people in Arizona and held other revival meetings across the country. In 1974, a traffic accident took him to Heaven, which seemed to have no cause. When he returned from

Heaven, he was entirely healed and continued for years to bring healing to others. Upon returning to life on the earth, Richard preached the gospel in many countries with many known evangelists, and on television and radio. He authored *My Time in Heaven: A True Story of Dying and Coming Back.*

CHAPTER 9

IN REALMS OF GLORY

William Smith

Bill was adopted as an infant, but he didn't find out until he was eighteen years of age. This explained why, from the time he was a young child, he had a deep, deep longing to know God as his Father.

One day I walked into my room, lay down on the bed, and began praying as usual. All of a sudden the ceiling disappeared. All I could see were swirling clouds of splendor and glory in fiery yellow, pink, and red. I was hearing a sound like a nuclear fission of extreme power. I was overcome with wanting to know what this was. An expanse opened above me. As I watched, it came down over top of me. I was fearful and trembling. A huge all-consuming cloud came toward me. The whole experience was terrifying. I could feel my heart racing, but there was nothing I could do. I was praying to God to tell me whatever this was and what was happening. I was still in my room looking up, but there was no longer any ceiling.

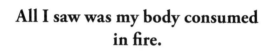

All I saw was my body consumed in fire.

I was now in a spiritual dimension. All I saw was my body consumed in fire. The whirlwind cloud had a sound, like a humming atomic power vibration—very loud, like a cosmic power sound. It was so powerful sounding that the energy of it scared me enough that I thought I would die. It was as if I was looking at a video of a nuclear explosion in slow speed so that I could see the strong ethereal electric nuclear power of it. All I could do was watch and listen. As I listened, I also heard a sound like a CD playing a song that I had written, *Run, Run into the Son.* I've always composed songs, and I had written that song to the Lord. It was my favorite, and now it was playing in my spirit.

The cloud of fire went to my feet and started moving upward. I saw this with my spiritual eyes, not my natural eyes because this was all happening in the spirit realm.

The red and orange fire moved up my legs. I couldn't see my body after it reached my torso, to my chest and throat and my arms. My entire body disappeared in the power of it. I was in my body watching it. I was perplexed as to how to stay alive. The cloud was consuming my whole body. The force came to my face. When it touched my face, my heart stopped beating. I knew my body was rock solid still. Like a dead person. A voice spoke into my right ear and said, "This is death." At that instant, I smelled roses like they were everywhere. I had no fear. I had no physical reaction, but I was purely alive—and fully discerning.

Just before I entered death, before my body stopped functioning, I knew it was impossible to escape what was going to happen. I knew how to hold my breath, almost to black out, as I was a diver. I thought, *I used to breathe, but now I'm not breathing air.* I was alive and breathing in the cloud stuff. I was breathing the spiritual power. As I was contemplating how to survive this encounter with all-powerful God, I simply died. It was a miracle that I still had full consciousness.

At the moment of death, the song kept playing. The only thing that kept me in my right mind was the song. At the same time, the Spirit of God was entirely in control. There was no confusion or chaos. He completely encompassed me and had taken over my entire being. Once I learned I was still alive on the other side, I had peace.

————— ◦◊◦ —————

Once I knew I was dead, all I wanted was to be with Jesus and the Father.

————— ◦◊◦ —————

While all this was going on, the words of my song, *Run, Run into the Son,* were coming out of the depths of my heart. They were the only things I heard except the voice in my right ear that said, "This is death." Death is final, terminating all I knew on earth. I was then so surrounded by such glory and power that I didn't think about anyone or anything. There was nothing that I missed on earth. I had no recollection of anything except the song. Once I knew I was dead, all I wanted was to be with Jesus and the Father.

SLOW MOTION

Now I was moving in slow motion to some degree, not fast, and was again aware of the song being played. It got louder as I was going upward. I had the distinct sense of moving upward, in a direction closer to the Source of life. Direction is hard to figure out in the eternal realm, but I was definitely heading upward, to a place above, to a higher spiritual place, to where God is. My consciousness at that point went from inside my body and all of my self-awareness to outside myself, to God. There was no more of the self-life inside me. Now Life was all around me, and I was moving into it—I was moving into God! I am describing what takes place in the spiritual realm, though at the time I did not have a complete understanding of what was taking place.

At this point there was no more hiddenness in my soul. Though I didn't completely understand it then, what took place is that I had escaped the imprisonment of my soul and was free to be part of what was outside myself in the spiritual realm. I was brought to being selfless. Now I was into myriads of the works that are in God that are stored above from before the foundation of the world. The day you die, you'll see that He's always been there. He's there immediately, even if you don't know it. You have no idea in this life on earth how much God is all over and around you all the time. He's always there.

What happened next? I saw the heavens open; and I saw the wheels that Ezekiel saw, though I did not see the beings in the wheel that he saw. In front of me appeared a huge array of wheels and lights that were spinning and sparkling. The splendor, the explosive sparkling, the flames of fire and glory, were all ablaze with millions of colors I had never seen before. The wheels stopped between me and the cosmic lights. The stopping point was arrayed in glory and wonder and flashing and peals of thunder. It all moved in such explosiveness.

The Wheels

It didn't make sense to me at first. They were more like wheeling clouds than wheels we have on earth. The Holy Spirit is in the wheels. The wheels have a lot to do with the spinning of the universe, and it all happens musically. The truth of God is the majesty of God and the wonder of God, which is the truth of God, and it all goes round and round. Together they create a symphony of glorious sounds. Inside the spinning comes an additional symphony.

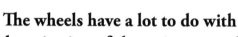

The wheels have a lot to do with the spinning of the universe, and it all happens musically.

Inside the wheel are multiple personalities, angels, and people. I tried to ascend the wheel of music. The wheel stops at the Father and remains stationary, but the wheels keep turning and all the voices start spinning and all the voices around the Father are in majestic harmony. That's the real purpose of the wheels, to open up the celestial music of the spheres. There is spatial direction through the music.

The wheels are not for transport from one place to another as we see on earth. For example, on earth we get on a bus to go somewhere, like to a concert. The earthly bus travels down the streets and maybe across a bridge or through a tunnel to take us to our destination. But once we get in the heavenly bus within the wheels, we're already there! I was in this moving thing that had everything already in it. I was no longer going to a concert, I was *in* a concert! In the heavenly realm, all sound joins in a galactic song as the wheels emerge in a musical expansion of sound.

In a way I cannot explain, I could see His glory and His greatness in the music. The music is to sing the truth. It is pure spiritual joy, uncontainable joy. The spiritual attainment of paradise is in the music of God. I saw friends and cities and angels in Heaven, but what was most amazing is the music. All of creation spins on a huge galactic never-ending song. The identity of everyone and everything is in the music. I don't want to compromise the spiritual perfection as I try to describe it.

WELCOME HOME

Leaving that atmosphere, I went into a great big orb of white sparkling light. I saw in the backdrop a huge, spatial blue ball, peaceful yet absorbing my full attention. There was much more than I could understand as it was way beyond my ability to comprehend or come close to the light orb. It was of another dimension. I wanted to go there. I wanted to go to the deepest place.

I had just gone through the celestial bliss of hearing His music and it was totally exhausting in the sense of being overwhelmed, somewhat like when Daniel saw the angel Gabriel or when John saw Jesus and fell at His feet in the third heaven, overwhelmed in His presence. The Father wasn't going to put me into all that cosmic energy and not let me wind down.

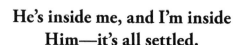

He's inside me, and I'm inside Him—it's all settled.

What I experienced was more than exterior glory—it was Him on the inside of me. After He showed me what He had in the wheels, He brought me to a place of peacefulness where it was just me and Him. His love for me was just about Him and me at that point, about His heart and me being inside Him and a spiritual peace and a profound sense of "Welcome home." That's what the blue was all about. He's inside me, and I'm inside Him—it's all settled. There's nothing more to be accomplished.

He wanted me to visualize Him as the Lord God Almighty, Creator and Everlasting Father. I saw that His power and glory and radiance is spiritual sovereignty, harmony, unity, and righteousness. There is a difference in the two identifiable characters who are one and the same God, one comes out of the other. The Spiritual

Person who unites each one, God's Spirit, moves from the Son to the Father. There is no separation between them. We finally see Jesus as who He is, wrapped up in unity with the Father. There's God Himself—single, only one. He reveals Himself in time through the incarnation. Jesus is all that comes from the Father.

When I went inside Him, I became part of His love. He serenaded me and sang me to His throne. I saw that He was my song and Lord God and Savior. It was not to see Him as much as to know Him and hear Him. To me it was more important than looking at Him. I saw His righteousness, His radiant, sovereign glory. I saw the Spiritual God Almighty! I didn't see the nail-scarred hands, but I did see His spiritual power.

The Throne Room

The throne room was filled with His own glory, the glory of spectacular God and His beauty and radiance. On the inside of His character was love, and His redeeming characteristic grabbed me and pulled me in like a loving father cares for his child. God Eternal spoke to my soul as if I were the only one. Indeed, if you are His, He will speak to you the very same way one glorious day.

The music became a spiritual display, with a host of angels dancing together around Him, glorifying Him. I understood somehow that it is my inheritance to be playing music to Him, coming to Him, singing to Him, and laying my life before Him. This is what I wanted. I thought I wanted the Father and Jesus, but then I saw in my heart that *He* wanted me to be there, He wanted to show me that *He* was giving me a gift. It wasn't about what I wanted, but what *He* wanted. I was part of the gift, and I was participating in the song He gave me. The way of Heaven, where there is no fear, is through praising Him.

In the quiet, I could hear voices but I couldn't see them. Yet I knew there were angels, myriads and myriads of angels. God wanted me to hear this more than see it. I had to hear Him to understand Him. To fall in love with Him, I had to hear Him. My music is part of my salvation. He was my song at first, and then He became my salvation.

Then Jesus took me into a deep blue vault, and I hovered inside it. He came to me and breathed on me—it was like water. It felt so peaceful and warm and tender. He held me inside His heart. Yet it was my Father's heart. Jesus brings us to the Father. He said to me, "In My Father's house are many mansions. I am the Way. You wanted to know the Father. If you see Me, you have seen the Father." It's not that I saw the Father. What I experienced was the voice and the love and His adoption of me. I knew I was conceived in the spiritual Kingdom under a genuine spirit of heavenly adoption.

————— ᧤᧤ᦐ —————

He held me inside His heart. Yet it was my Father's heart.

————— ᧤᧤ᦐ —————

He then lifted me up and said, "Whatever I whisper to you in the darkness, speak in the light; what I whisper in your ear, proclaim." There are hidden places, mysterious places where He has each of us in His heart, and He will speak to each one of us personally. I love to hear His voice. I'd rather have His Spirit and His voice than anything else. We can trust His voice. In His voice is the spiritual virtue, the abundant virtue of His kindness and love. I was engulfed in His heartfelt love, all the virtue of His heart. That's what you hear when He speaks to you.

The song, *Run, Run into the Son* was still playing, and when it approached that glorious realm, it became part of the flashing and the glory. My song hit the sparkling, and all of a sudden, in that area as big as Heaven, trillions of celestial sounds took my song and turned it into a Spirit-filled symphony. Now I was in a new realm, approaching the love of God. He had given me an original song. Now the Father was embracing me with His glory, and I was entirely overwhelmed and in complete bliss. All I saw was the glory surrounding the Lord, no image of His Person. There were glorious colors and explosive joy. It was absolute joy! As I got closer to the area of the throne, I saw beings and thought they were angels, but I never saw faces. To me they seemed like angels.

A circle appeared in the middle of His glory, then the light faded somewhat. It wasn't dark, just not as light as it had been. The area where I was standing became quiet and still. Then I felt wind, warmth, and breath like water pouring over me, saturating me. I was being picked up, then I was inside the circle. I heard a voice say, "I love you." It was at that very moment, I finally knew He was my Father; I understood that He was mine and I was His. He wanted to show me that He knew what I needed—a father—and that I wanted so much to know and see and hear Him as my Father.

In His Garden

Within a second after that, I was immediately moved over and placed in a garden—His garden. I saw shimmering water, golden-yellow transparent water, flowing down like liquid sunshine. Pure yellow gold was coming down from above. The entire atmosphere shimmered in golden light, like waves of heat shimmer. It came straight down and into the garden. God had put me in a tree, like a cat sitting on a branch. I had been through absolute bliss and a power transformation. He now wanted me to rest, so He put me in the tree. I watched the light for what seemed like six or seven hours.

Then suddenly I was back in His presence. I found myself thinking, *Do I want to go back?* He must have put that thought in my mind. *Do I **need** to go back? Is this my call and destiny?* He gave me the option because He knew I really wanted to share my experience with people on earth. It was so wonderful that I had to come back to tell people.

He asked me, "Do you want to go back to the earth?" I wanted to say no. I was disenchanted with the whole situation down here, but my response to Him, "I do want to show the earth who You are, what You said, and about this experience." In a matter of seconds, I was in my bed, sprawled out like I'd been flying. I was very tired. And amazed.

When I finally pulled myself together, I walked out to the living room and picked up my guitar and started worshiping. It was all I could do.

Commentary

Bill was adopted when he was only days old, and something always seemed to be missing inside him. He longed to know God as his Father even before he knew he was adopted. God took this young man who knew what adoption is in human terms and showed him the reality of what it is to be adopted by God—to be made fully His own, to be thoroughly and completely His, and to be entirely "home" and where he belongs. Bill knows now that his love for music is God's gift to him so that he might participate, even on the earth, in the magnificent glory of worship that permeates Heaven continually. The Bible says that *"God richly supplies us with all things to enjoy"* (1 Tim. 6:17)—so the giftings, abilities, and talents He has given us to enjoy are motivated by His personal love for us. And nothing will bring us more satisfaction and enjoyment than what brings God glory. Jonathan Edwards is quoted to have said, "God is most glorified in us when we are most satisfied in Him." To be in God's presence is to enjoy God and be fully satisfied in Him.

God allowed Bill to experience in the heavenly realm far beyond what most of us envision of Heaven. To speak with Bill is to speak with someone who has seen ultimate reality and knows it must function by love and truth. Bill's experience lifts us out of our earthbound images of Gentle Jesus with the lamb in His arms and causes us to see Him as entirely able to sovereignly take care of the affairs of planets and nations, while also caring for His own flock who are His—no matter what the challenge. He is our great Savior, Lord, and Lover of our souls.

Bill's experience gives us new revelation of the majesty of the humility of Jesus that He would leave behind all that is His in Heaven to take the place of a crucified Man so we could one day be with Him in all His glory. God took Bill to Heaven and allowed him to experience the enormity of His lordship in the universe, and His cosmic energy as the Almighty. He witnessed the absolute authority of God who sustains all that exists with the word of His power. That power extends to your own life. From the midst of all that overwhelming power flows the immeasurable tender, all-encompassing love of God that He showed to Bill in the most personal way, making Bill aware that God wanted to have him close to Him more than Bill ever wanted to know God as his Father. Imagine, the omnipotent God oh so tenderly loves you!

Yours, O Lord, is the greatness and the power and the glory and the victory and the majesty, indeed everything that is in the heavens and the earth; Yours is the dominion, O Lord, and You exalt Yourself as head over all (1 Chronicles 29:11).

About Bill Smith

Bill is a lover of God and a musician who writes and produces his own CDs of "Realms of Glory" in heavenly music. He shares the love of God in an effective prison ministry and wherever God leads him to bring blessings and His presence.

CHAPTER 10

EXPERIENCING HEAVEN, EXPERIENCING HELL

Richard Eby, MD

Richard Eby was a baby who should never have been born. His mother was found to have no reproductive organs and was declared barren. But being a woman of great faith, she prayed a prayer like Hannah's prayer in First Samuel chapter 1 and asked for a son. Soon she found herself pregnant and dedicated the baby to Messiah's use. But six months into the pregnancy, the fetus died and she miscarried. The obstetrician was about to declare the fetus dead, after some fifteen minutes, when the baby gasped and began to breathe. He grew up in a home of great faith, believing that if he needed help, Jesus was there to supply it.

> *But then at age 60, his life was snuffed out*
> *in a second.*

A week after my 60th birthday, while cleaning out the attic, I was about to take a heavy carton downstairs and outside to the trash when a small voice told me to drop the box off a second story balcony so I didn't have to carry it all the way down. Thinking it was the Lord's voice, I quickly went to the balcony. As I leaned against the railing, it gave way and I plunged two stories to the cement sidewalk below—head first.

The eggshell of my skull completely broke apart and broke the large blood vessel of my brain; my eyes popped out; and then my body ricocheted into a bush. I bled out from the blood vessel and was a bloodless corpse hanging upside down on a bush when they found me. I was dead on impact, but the emergency medical technicians had to take me to a hospital to legally declare me dead. It was ten hours before there was any evidence of life.

Immediately, upon dying I experienced no pain because there is no pain in death. There is an immediate transfer to the spirit body, which is what keeps our physical bodies alive. But when the spirit separates from the physical body, the separation is called death. It's the release from all suffering, sorrow, and all grief and pain—if you go immediately to Heaven, that is. We have a natural instinct to want to stay alive. If we were without a fear of death, we and animal life in general, would self-destruct. But that is eliminated once we are dead.

Everything changes when your life on earth is over. There is no time between the moment of death and where we arrive—either in Heaven or in hell. Instantly, with a thud, I arrived at a place that was so ecstatically loaded with love, I knew it was Heaven, though I didn't know *where* in Heaven at first. Heaven is so blissful that it is beyond human description. To be in Heaven is to be released from all physical difficulties that our bodies register upon the mind.

I was instantly in Messiah, *in Him.*

There's no time between being here and there, no floating around, you're instantly in Heaven. It's so far beyond any human words. There is total love, total confidence, total peace; everything is perfect. This will be hard for people on earth to understand, but I was instantly in Messiah, *in Him.* It's spiritual because bone and flesh cannot inherit the Kingdom. Therefore, we can't be there in earthly material. I knew I was me, and yet I was in Messiah.

There is no fear in Heaven. Fear was reduced to zero after Jesus died, when He arranged a place of total joy and peace. As long as we are in the flesh, we have built-in fear. God put it in there so people would have a form of fear so they wouldn't voluntarily hurt themselves. In Heaven, there is no such thing as flesh as we know it. It's entirely spiritual. What God can do is limitless because it's a spiritual material. We have so many senses in the spirit body, unlike the five senses we have here on earth. And all those senses are in total ecstasy. The same mind you have there is the same mind that Messiah has.

Spiritual Reality

Instantly upon landing, I looked to see what I landed on. My feet were the same size and shape. I recognized myself by the conformity to my earthly self. My spirit eyes saw it all. I could see right through my spiritual body. No weight. No pain, fright, or discomfort. Just joy. And no bones, ligaments, or organs in our spiritual bodies. There is no material I can describe in words for our spirits. It is the form that God created to provide life for the flesh. Once that is removed, it has to go somewhere, either Heaven or hell.

The first thing I realized is that I did not have the mind I had on earth. Here on earth, life is the product of brain tissues. When the body is gone, it seems that we suddenly have an electronic chip of the mind of the Lord Jesus implanted in our minds. We know more information than all of our brains here on earth. Suddenly, I had a mind that thought with a speed incomputable on earth.

The first time I heard the Lord's voice, He said, "Dick, you're dead." Though I heard the voice within me, it was the voice of the King of kings and Lord of lords. His voice was absolutely indescribable. His saying it was judicial, authoritative, loving, humble, kind, and accurate all at once. That He called me by my name showed me the intimacy He has with my existence. I asked, "Why do you call me Dick?" He said, "When I died for you on the cross, it was a most intimate thing. When you accepted Me, you became a new person and part of My body for whom I will be coming soon." We had quite a conversation while I was with Jesus.

It is mind-to-mind talk there. The need of air to transmit sound and for the ear to hear is absent in Heaven. There is nothing in the physics of Heaven that is similar to the physics on earth. He was speaking inside my mind and I was answering with a rapidity that can only be imagined. The language is so perfect that instantly I realized each word in a split second. Timing was perfection. It meant only one thing. He knew exactly what He wanted me to know. If I asked a question, He had the answer ready before I even asked it.

———— Ꮼ ————

Jesus and I walked in Heaven together, but it was more like flying than walking.

———— Ꮼ ————

Jesus and I walked in Heaven together, but it was more like flying than walking. We were talking while suspended in midair. There is no weight or gravity in Heaven, so there is no need to touch the ground. As we were conversing, He added little bits of data to increase my knowledge, and when I would ask questions, he always had the answers. Communication is so far superior than anything we can imagine down here. Space is also limitless. I asked Him a question about how large an area designated for different persons would be and He answered, "I only give them the desires of their heart. I put it in my book. Didn't you read My book? Everything in it is explanatory of what a child of Mine needs to know." Several times I asked a question and He answered, "Didn't you read My book?"

LOVE IN A DIFFERENT DIMENSION

His love is in a different dimension than our idea of love. There is no question of His love. Human intelligence is inadequate to understand the love of our Creator, which was known the moment I was with Him. But I was also "in" Him. In the spirit, we are what the Scriptures say—we are in Him and He is in us (see Gal. 2:20). Yet we don't lose our identity. The love He infused me with instantly upon my arrival was so much more complete than we can experience on earth. Our flesh is always standing in the way. Even if He tried to give us a full dose here on earth, we would diminish its intensity by our unbelief because we couldn't believe it's that good. When we are in Heaven, though, it seems normal that He wants to bring us a full dose of His love and peace. Everything seems normal, yet magnificently limitless. The only definition is Heaven is all about God!

There are no languages on the face of the earth that can adequately describe a place that is indescribable. I landed in a vast valley with thousands of flowers, all different kinds. The trees of Heaven are huge, nothing exactly as on earth, because it's all made of a material that is indestructible, the same as our spirit bodies. Nothing like sin or fire can ever touch Heaven. God made it for His own throne room.

The light in Heaven would blind our natural eyes immediately. He is the Sun of Heaven. With spiritual eyes I could see any distance and through anything. Blades of grass are not broken when I walked on them. There are no insect bites. Leaves on trees do not turn brown because there is no death. There is only the absolute spiritual divinity that God used to create His own home.

The odor of Heaven was a sweet-smelling savor. The aroma came from the prayers of the saints who are in Heaven, not on earth. The prayers of those who were saved and are worshiping and praising God in Heaven are so sweet smelling to the Lord that He allows them to smell their own prayers. The sacrifices of animals in the Old Testament produced a barbecue kind of smell that to His nostrils was sweet smelling because they were doing what He told them to do as forerunners of the sacrifice of His Son.

Then He didn't talk to me anymore. The trip was over.

I thought I was there permanently, but suddenly I whizzed through a long valley and up a great canyon where I heard my wife's voice. I heard her calling "Dick." God permitted me to hear her as she was praying, and then everything went dead as I was returned into my body. I found myself completely unconscious from then on. The body had never left, and my spirit was back in it. My wife asked the Lord to send me back—and He did. The exit from Heaven was instantaneous, faster than the speed of light.

At first there was no blood in my body. As a corpse, I was aware that the room was filled with a brilliant light. I said, "Lord, I'm aware of a terrific light. Yet I know I'm not alive." He said, "Yes, I'm putting life back in your body, and you will be able to resume your medical practice."

With my doctor's mind I asked Him how He decided which organs to restore first. He said, "My son, no one has ever asked Me that before. I'll tell you." Then He went from up my legs to my arms, then into my chest activating this and that. Then He said, "My son, I'll be leaving now."

Then He was gone, and I was alive again.

Five years later, I was in Israel visiting Lazarus' tomb, which is like a small cave. The cave holds three people; two ladies were there with me. All of a sudden, the lights went out. We were two stories underground. It was a terrible darkness. Both women screamed. I said, "Don't scream, just pray."

Then I was alone in absolute blackness, and suddenly I was bathed in a limitless and powerful light. I knew instantly that I had to be in my spirit body. Standing beside me was a fantastically beautiful human figure—it was Jesus. He was slightly taller than I, about six foot. He must have stood slightly above most of His colleagues in Israel. I looked into a face so magnificent that it cannot be described. Absolute divinity, merciful yet judicial. A slight smile was on His face as if He was enjoying this moment. He put His arm around me so that it permeated me in a hug of love. I knew it was about something important happening.

Jesus spoke to me as He had five years earlier. He said, "My son, I'm going to show you hell."

I replied, "I believe in You. That's off limits."

He said, "I want to show you a holding tank for those who refuse to believe in Me."

"I don't want to go."

"I'll take you there for two minutes. I'll send My Spirit with you."

"But my name is in the Book of Life," I said.

He responded, "I've expunged it for two minutes. For that time, you will feel what it is like in hell." I knew I would experience the worst that anyone had, even an atheist. An atheist doesn't believe in God but he has to. Hell is separation from the very Person in charge of the universe. Jesus said He would explain what was happening.

I said, "Get it over with as long as You will put my name back."

FALLING INTO HELL

I felt myself falling. I fell straight down and stopped at the center of the earth in an enclosed pit or chamber that was about ten feet high by four feet square. It had no exit or entrance. I was in total silence, total darkness. He gave me just enough of the five senses to realize these things. I cried out to Jesus, "You said You'd explain." He answered, "Yes, My son. You are in a place of total isolation prepared for the demons. Absence of God results in no light, no sound, and no heat."

I would have gone stark raving mad if the love of God hadn't been with me. Then He removed the five senses normal to the fleshly body and gave me what is normal to the spirit body—it feels like a million senses to the spirit body. They are limitless. Place, time, speed.

The spirit of man that came out of God originally has no limitations. The absence of God means no light because God is light.

Just like He said, I was in a holding tank for sinners until the great white throne of judgment takes place. It was so terrible that I find it hard to describe. I had gone right through the center of the earth, just buzzed right into a stone tomb in the holding tank. I was terrified. Voices tell the sinners why they are there, how they got there. There's no escape; and it's an instant thing—when a sinner dies, that person is there instantly.

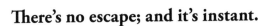

There's no escape; and it's instant.

It is terrifying beyond description. I smelled the stink of demons. I banged on walls wanting out. I was surrounded by a thousand little bodies like deformed cats and dogs. They were chained. Behind their eyes was fire. Their intent was to harass me and terrorize me. The floor was covered with a thousand demons. I didn't have to count them, I just knew how many there were. They were the size of little spiders. They looked up at me and in the most terrible language, far worse than any on earth, they began ridiculing me for turning down the Savior so I was now there with them. They said, "We'll never let you out. We'll give you the hell we're experiencing."

They crawled up the side walls of this cavity and around my face and then they started a concert. I had never heard anything like it on earth. So loud, so haunting, obscene words and language I would not repeat. They continued to taunt me, thinking I had died and gone to hell, "You got here because you turned down the death of Jesus on the earth." They continued, "Why did you think there was an earthquake when Jesus died on the cross? It was to make the nails in His hands hurt worse. The terrible black cloud—that was us demons. Satan had us come and paralyze what God was planning to do so there could never be salvation."

I asked, "Why are you in hell?" They said, "We had already accepted Satan as our savior and we had no choice. We're here forever and we'll never let you out." The stench was absolute death because Satan is the inventor of death. The demons were enjoying it because they knew nothing else.

THE WHITE THRONE

Then I was snatched out of there and placed before a white throne. The Spirit was still with me or I wouldn't have gotten out of hell. I said, "Jesus I want to see the loving eyes of my heavenly Father."

Again He said, "My son, didn't you read my book? To look at my Father's face would destroy you." Then He said, "There is a white throne and there is a time of judgment, and He is the Righteous Judge. He will not allow a verdict to be decided until they've had their day in court."

I saw a book in His hands and in Hebrew it said, "The Lamb's Book of Life." With lightning speed He was turning pages and looking for my name. The Lord said, "He's looking for your name." The book was closed with a clap of thunder. Jesus said, "Your name is not in there. I've expunged it to show you there is such a book and it will be looked at by My heavenly Father."

Then suddenly I was back in Lazarus' tomb, the light came on, and the two ladies were with me again.

Now Jesus was still speaking to me mind to mind. He said, "I went there first before you were born and I took the keys to hell and death." He went on to say, "I had to form a new place that would be in total isolation from God." I asked why. He answered, "Because that was the desire of their hearts. The only way people can get into hell is by their own volition. I've given each person a will. The desire of the hearts of those who will not accept Me is that they want Us to stay out of the way. They don't want the Father, the Son, or the Holy Spirit. They say, 'Leave me alone, I'll make it.' They think they can make their own lives, live the way they want. That's the will of people who deprive themselves of salvation. So I immediately had to create a place of total separation."

People on earth do not have much time to waste.

Jesus had taken my place when He died for my sins and He wanted me to see what would have happened if I hadn't taken Him as my Savior. He said it very clearly: "When I'm sitting beside the Father, unless you confess Me before others, I am tongue-tied by your action. Unless you confess before men that you have taken Me as your Savior, I cannot turn to My Father and say, 'This man has accepted Me as his Advocate.' There is soon coming a day when all the prophecies will have been fulfilled. People on earth do not have much time to waste. All they have to do is accept Me." He said, "I'm simply showing you that your spirit body is not restricted by the earth."

Then I heard gorgeous music. I realized this music was entirely different from anything I had ever heard. I stood there letting it bathe me. I don't know how long I was listening. It was the first time I ever knew something so beautiful could exist. It was not vocal or instrumental, it was heavenly. It was different. It is impossible to cut up eternity with beats, which is about time. There is no time in Heaven. Eternity is timeless. On earth, music is regulated by beats because it's all about time.

I asked Jesus, "What is eternity?" He answered, "It's now."

We move in time here on earth, where our whole lives are regulated by the time the earth circulates around the sun. Jesus is the same yesterday, today, and tomorrow. In Heaven, our lives are released from the confines of time. When we hit the shores of Paradise, we are no longer bound by time. It's also part of our salvation. Even now, when we are deep in prayer and in concert with Him, we forget about time.

Jesus said, "Tell them that when I created man I gave him a will, and I will not override it. I made him with the necessity of following and worshiping. The choice is Myself or the adversary, the devil. Tell them if they choose Me as their Lord and Master, it's free. When I hung on that cross and I said, 'It is finished,' I was not kidding." He used the word kidding because when He had showed Himself to me in the hospital to bring me back to life, I still had a dead and bloodless body. I reacted as a doctor and said, "You must be kidding." He told me He was not kidding when He died and there's nothing left except to accept it.

Tell them, "Get rid of the pride that is between them and their Creator. Unless they do this soon, it will be too late. I am ready to return as soon as My Father says it's time. What you saw happens to be the first death. I had overlooked the second hell that burns forever. The antithesis of Heaven is the pit of hell."

The horror of being out of relationship with God is to be totally isolated in hell. I felt it with my hands and my feet. Those who don't believe it don't want to believe anything.

Don't go to bed tonight thinking that all this doesn't exist—it does.

That's the message I have to tell.

...Choose for yourselves today whom you will serve... (Joshua 24:15).

Set your mind on the things above, not on the things that are on earth. For you have died and your life is hidden with Christ in God. When Christ, who is our life, is revealed, then you also will be revealed with Him in glory (Colossians 3:2-4).

Commentary

Heaven is a wonderful place, but there is the reality of hell as well for those who do not accept what Jesus did on the cross to pay for their sins. If someone is brain dead for even a few minutes, they are considered a vegetable. Dr. Eby was dead for ten hours. Nothing short of an incredible miracle could have put him back together so that he was completely whole.

I (Sid) interviewed Dr. Eby at age 86, and he was still completely well and still telling people what Jesus instructed him to tell them. His testimony presents us with a choice, for those who have not already made the choice. What could you be waiting for? The facts are there. It's Jesus and Heaven, or hell and demons. Accepting Jesus means acknowledging that you need a Savior—someone to save you from the consequences of your sin and from living independently from God. Only someone perfect could be your substitute and only Jesus was the perfect, sinless Son of God. I urge you to consider this very carefully. It is the most important decision you will ever make in your life.

About Dr. Richard Eby

After his experience in Heaven, Dr. Eby continued his medical practice for a time, but soon gave it up to travel and tell people the message Jesus had given him to share and to tell of his experiences in Heaven and hell. A great many people came to the Lord as a result of his testimony. Dr. Eby lived a healthy life into his 90s and is now in Heaven with Jesus.

CONCLUSION

WHAT ABOUT YOUR HEAVEN EXPERIENCE?

It doesn't seem real. I can't even relate to the man I was. Before I met Jesus, I was a Jew who did not even know for sure if there was a God. And if there was one, I didn't know if He was interested in me as an individual. I did not know what would happen if I died. I just assumed I would cease to exist. I did not know there was a real Heaven. I did not know God would answer prayer. I did not know God would speak to me. I did not know I could experience His tangible presence.

The Bible says you become a new creation when you believe in Jesus (see 2 Cor. 5:17). That's the way I feel. The old Sid Roth does not even exist. When I had my experience with my Messiah Jesus more than forty years ago, my spirit became brand-new.

Man consists of three parts—spirit, soul, and body. The spirit is our contact with God who is a Spirit. Our soul is our mind and emotions, and our body is our "earth suit." It took many years for my mind to be renewed to understand the invisible world. Although my earth suit is older and has a new color roof—gray instead of blonde—my spirit has gained the ascendency over my soul and body.

Life is like an iceberg. Ninety percent is under the water, invisible to the naked eye. The only way to understand the supernatural world is through the Bible. I don't know how I existed without knowing God, or living in His love 24/7, or experiencing His peace no matter what the circumstances, or gaining His wisdom in all of life's choices. I can honestly say I now have no fear of lack, sickness, or even death.

If you do not know Him before you die, Heaven will not be your home.

If you do not know God before you die, you will not know Him after you die. I did not say *believe* in Him but *know* Him. *If you do not know Him before you die, Heaven will not be your home.*

I woke up a few nights ago saying three times, "Jesus is coming soon! Jesus is coming soon! Jesus is coming soon!" I believe this with all my heart. And the truth is, none of us know when our end will come.

The first step to knowing God is to ask Him for forgiveness of sin. Heaven is a perfect utopia. No sin is possible there. We all have sinned, and sinful people cannot enter Heaven. This is why God sent Jesus to die for our sins and by His sacrifice God wipes our slates clean. When we are clean, God can touch our spirits with His life.

After you pray for this wonderful God exchange, start reading your Bible and become part of a group of believers (congregation). This will help your spirit gain ascendency.

If you have never received this gift of forgiveness for your sins and you want the promise of knowing God, say the following prayer out loud. There is a supernatural power in the spoken word.

Dear God, I have committed many sins in my life (name them, such as lying, stealing, abortion, sex outside of marriage, addictions, pornography, dabbling in New Age religions or activities, etc.). I am so sorry, and I now turn from them. I know You will give me the power to turn away from sin. I believe Jesus died for all my sins, and by His blood I am forgiven. In fact, according to Your Word, You remember them no more. Now that I am clean, I make Jesus my Messiah and ask You to live inside me. Amen.

If you said this prayer for the first time or you want to know more about this supernatural life, please visit my Website designed especially for you. Well, I really designed it for Jewish people who do not know Jesus. But it gives all people a deep faith of understanding and answers your questions:

www.theythoughtforthemselves.com.

To grow in the supernatural, start watching my television show, *It's Supernatural!* I have years of archived programs that you can watch for free on my Web page, www.SidRoth.org. My passion is to mentor you so that you can do the same works as Jesus.

And now I want to bless you with a supernatural prayer that God taught Moses to pray over the Jewish people. God promised as a result that His name would be on them and bless them. This is my New Covenant version of Numbers 6:24-26:

The Lord has already blessed you and kept you because Jesus is your Messiah and Lord. The Lord has smiled upon you and has already gifted you. The Lord has already surrounded you with His favor and given you His shalom, His peace or completeness, in your spirit, soul, and body. I seal you in the Name of Yeshua Ha Maschiach T'sidkeno, Jesus the Messiah, our Righteousness.

Shalom and love,
SID ROTH

CONTACT INFORMATION

Sid Roth

info@SidRoth.org
www.SidRoth.org
www.TheyThoughtForThemselves.com

Lonnie Lane

lonnie@lonnielane.com
www.SidRoth.org (Articles)
www.TheyThoughtForThemselves.com
www.lonnielane.blogspot.com

Dean Braxton

www.DeanBraxton.com

Ian and Michael McCormack

True229@gmail.com
www.aglimpseofeternity.org

Jubilee Mitchell

PO Box 195
Maryville, IL 62062
Mitchellrhoda@hotmail.com

Robert Misst

29 Secoia Crescent
Mangere, Manukau
Auckland 2022, New Zealand
ramisst@yahoo.com

Richard Sigmund

To order his book, write to:
Cleft of the Rock Ministries
615 5th Street
Maxwell, IA 50161

William Smith

Jesuscosmos@yahoo.com

Gary Wood

Garywoodmi@aol.com
www.GaryWoodMinistries.com

Khalida Wukawitz

KhalidaJesusLove@Yahoo.com

Contact Information for Sid Roth's *It's Supernatural!* and Messianic Vision

Mailing Address
PO Box 39222
Charlotte, NC 28278

Telephone
704-943-6500

Fax
704-943-6501

Website
www.sidroth.org

Email
info@sidroth.org

Messianic Vision Canada
Suite 143
5929 L Jeanne D'Arc Blvd
Orleans, Ontario KLC 7K2

Email
Canada@sidroth.org

IN THE RIGHT HANDS, THIS BOOK WILL CHANGE LIVES!

Most of the people who need this message will not be looking for this book. To change their lives, you need to put a copy of this book in their hands.

> *But others (seeds) fell into good ground, and brought forth fruit, some a hundred-fold, some sixty-fold, some thirty-fold* (Matthew 13:8).

Our ministry is constantly seeking methods to find the good ground, the people who need this anointed message to change their lives. Will you help us reach these people?

> *Remember this—a farmer who plants only a few seeds will get a small crop. But the one who plants generously will get a generous crop* (2 Corinthians 9:6).

EXTEND THIS MINISTRY BY SOWING
3 BOOKS, 5 BOOKS, 10 BOOKS, **OR MORE TODAY,**
AND BECOME A LIFE CHANGER!

Thank you,

Don Nori Sr., Founder
Destiny Image
Since 1982

DESTINY IMAGE PUBLISHERS, INC.

"Promoting Inspired Lives."

VISIT OUR NEW SITE HOME AT
WWW.DESTINYIMAGE.COM

FREE SUBSCRIPTION TO DI NEWSLETTER

Receive free unpublished articles by top DI authors, exclusive

discounts, and free downloads from our best and newest books.

Visit www.destinyimage.com to subscribe.

Write to: Destiny Image
                   P.O. Box 310
                   Shippensburg, PA 17257-0310

Call: 1-800-722-6774

Email: orders@destinyimage.com

For a complete list of our titles or to place an order
online, visit www.destinyimage.com.

FIND US ON FACEBOOK OR FOLLOW US ON TWITTER.

www.facebook.com/destinyimage   **facebook**
www.twitter.com/destinyimage   **twitter**